Happy 1st Birthday
Jacob xxx Howie & Rebecca

The Macmillan
TREASURY
of NURSERY
RHYMES *and*
POEMS

To all my family – A.C.

The Macmillan
TREASURY
of NURSERY
RHYMES *and*
POEMS

With a foreword by

ROGER McGOUGH

Illustrated by

ANNA CURREY

Edited by

ALISON GREEN

MACMILLAN
CHILDREN'S BOOKS

First published in 1998 by Macmillan Children's Books
A division of Macmillan Publishers Limited
25 Eccleston Place, London SW1W 9NF
and Basingstoke
Associated companies around the world.

ISBN 0 333 74165 X

1 3 5 7 9 8 6 4 2

A CIP catalogue record for this book is available from the British Library.

Colour reproduction by Speedscan Ltd

Printed and bound in Great Britain by
Butler & Tanner Ltd, Frome and London

Contents

Wakey, Wakey!
Poems to Start the Day

Skyscraper, Skyscraper

Poems about Town

Squelching in My Shoes
Countryside Poems

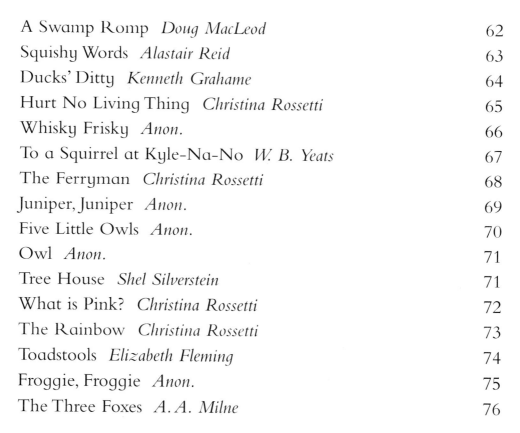

Look out Stomach, Here it Comes!

Poems about Food

"Purr," says the Cat
Poems for Pets and Friends

Babies are Funny
Poems about Families

One, Two, Buckle My Shoe
Counting Poems

Mudpie Stew
Garden Poems

If You Should Meet a Crocodile

Poems about Wild Animals

If I Were a Queen
Royal Poems

How Many Miles to Babylon?
Poems about Journeys

I Can Tie My Shoelace

Poems about Me

I'm a Little Teapot

Action Rhymes

Quack! Quack! Quack!

🪶 *Farmyard Poems* 🪶

Do Your Ears Hang Low?

🌼 *Nonsense Poems and Tongue-Twisters* 🌼

The North Wind Doth Blow

Poems about the Weather

Don't go Looking for Fairies
Magical and Spooky Poems

Star Light, Star Bright
Poems for Bedtime

Foreword

I had an exceedingly favoured childhood. I could step outside the back of my house into a large garden that ran down to a babbling stream. There was a tree-house and a swing as well as a unicorn. Beyond the gaily painted fence was a forest inhabited by goblins, above which rose a range of blue mountains and on top of the highest perched a castle, its crystal turrets reflecting the sun's golden rays.

This, of course, was the childhood of my imagination. The reality was bleaker, the back-to-back terraced houses of Liverpool in the 1940s. A scarred landscape of bombed sites and air-raid shelters. Much of the time, that reality itself was exciting and stimulating, but when the shadows closed in I would retreat into that infinite world of the imagination.

My earliest memories of poetry are of listening to nursery rhymes and speaking them aloud with my mother.

Pictures came into my head of quacklesome ducks and deranged dragons, shaped and coloured by the heartbeat of the rhythm and the comforting expectancy of the rhymes. And then came the books in which shared looking and saying was the beginning of reading. Everyday and familiar objects named and spoken which was the beginning of language. Through poetry my vocabulary was enriched and I developed skills to use words in a particular way.

"Poetry is language drawing attention to itself", and the sooner parents introduce poetry the sooner children can utilise it, for it will be seen as part of the whole world, not something dry or separate. Children are open to poetry, to that irrepressible charge of language, and it is adults who are responsible for making them think it is difficult or dull.

Centuries ago, in many parts of the world, music, poetry and dance were normally one and the same art, and in young children they still are, until poetry becomes something to read in silence. (The Poetry of Shush, rather than the Poetry of Share.) A child will not make the distinction between the spoken and the written. Language is "stuff" that can be shaped and arranged to make you laugh or cry. Where words collide, children sense its fizzing power, the magic that it can unleash.

Older readers go straight for meaning and disregard (or have become blind to) poetic patterns. But the child is a wide-eyed explorer in the rich jungle of language. To read poetry is to dawdle, to wander away from the main road and daydream.

> Sometimes they trap me
> Stop me in my tracks
>
> Thinking my way through
> Towards a promising idea
>
> When I am distracted
> By a sound. A spelling crackles.
>
> Without a second thought
> I am off into the thicket

(from *Word Trap*)

Part of the fun of poetry for the young is that while everybody is encouraging them to read quickly, the poet encourages them to read slowly. In fact children are born with the gift of reading slowly enough, not to have to slow down.

As a child I used to mumble in a Liverpool accent and so was sent to elocution lessons where I learned to mumble louder and more clearly. Again, the key was poetry and I revelled in the sound of words even if I didn't always understand their meaning.

Children's verse has by its very nature a propensity to be read aloud and so most of the poems you will find here are longing to be set free from the page.

The earliest anthologies that I remember were given to me at school and, to be honest, I found them worthy but dull, as did, I believe, the teachers. To have owned this Macmillan Treasury I would have swapped countless conkers, Dinky toys and even sweet coupons. Alison Green is an enthusiast who knows her poetry as well as her young audience, and this lovely, rich book will grow up with the child. I envy the young readers their choice and their appetite.

Roger McGough, 1998

Wakey, Wakey!

Poems to Start the Day

Good Morning
When It's Morning

Good morning when it's morning
Good night when it is night
Good evening when it's dark out
Good day when it is light
Good morning to the sunshine
Good evening to the sky
And when it's time to go away
Good-bye
Good-bye
Good-bye.

Mary Ann Hoberman

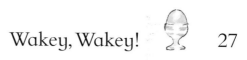

Waking Up

It's five in the morning,
I *know* it's not day.
But I am AWAKE
And I'm longing to play.
My toys are no fun
So I've thrown them all out.
I don't *think* my teddies
Will mind if I shout.
Oh! Look! It's my mummy!
Oh! Hello! Here's Dad.
Oh! . . .

   Is getting up now so *terribly* bad?

Lucy Coats

Wakey, Wakey!

Wakey, wakey, rise and shine.
Make your bed,
And then make mine.

Anon.

Time to Get Up

A birdie with a yellow bill
Hopped upon the window sill,
Cocked his shining eye and said:
"Aint you 'shamed, you sleepy-head?"

Robert Louis Stevenson

Elsie Marley

Elsie Marley is grown so fine,
She won't get up to feed the swine,
But lies in bed till eight or nine.
    Lazy Elsie Marley.

Anon.

The Cock Crows in the Morn

The cock crows in the morn
To tell us to rise,
And he that lies late
Will never be wise:
For early to bed,
And early to rise,
Is the way to be healthy
And wealthy and wise.

Anon.

Early Country Village Morning

Cocks crowing
Hens knowing
later they will cluck
their laying song

Houses stirring
a donkey clip-clopping
the first market bus
comes jugging along

Soon the sun will give a big yawn
and open her eye
pushing the last bit of darkness
out of the sky

Grace Nichols

Minnie and Winnie

Minnie and Winnie
Slept in a shell.
Sleep, little ladies!
And they slept well.

Pink was the shell within,
Silver without;
Sounds of the great sea
Wander'd about.

Sleep, little ladies!
Wake not soon!
Echo on echo
Dies to the moon.

Two bright stars
Peep'd into the shell.
"What are they dreaming of?
Who can tell?"

Started a green linnet
Out of the croft;
Wake, little ladies,
The sun is aloft!

Alfred, Lord Tennyson

Pippa's Song

The year's at the spring;
The day's at the morn;
Morning's at seven;
The hill-side's dew-pearled;
The lark's on the wing;
The snail's on the thorn;
God's in His heaven—
All's right with the world!

Robert Browning

Cat Kisses

Sandpaper kisses
on a cheek or a chin—
that is the way
for a day to begin!

Sandpaper kisses—
a cuddle, a purr.
I have an alarm clock
that's covered with fur.

Bobbi Katz

Singing-Time

I wake in the morning early
And always, the very first thing,
I poke out my head and I sit up in bed
And I sing and I sing and I sing.

Rose Fyleman

Sneezing

If you sneeze on Monday,
    you sneeze for danger;
Sneeze on a Tuesday,
    kiss a stranger;
Sneeze on a Wednesday,
    sneeze for a letter;
Sneeze on a Thursday,
    something better.
Sneeze on a Friday,
    sneeze for sorrow;
Sneeze on a Saturday,
    joy tomorrow.

Anon.

One Misty Moisty Morning

One misty moisty morning
     When cloudy was the weather,
There I met an old man
     Clothed all in leather;
Clothed all in leather,
     With cap under his chin,
How do you do, and how do you do,
     And how do you do again?

Anon.

Mary Ann

Mary Ann, Mary Ann,
Make the porridge in a pan;
Make it thick, make it thin,
Make it any way you can.

Anon.

Egg Thoughts (soft-boiled)

I do not like the way you slide,
I do not like your soft inside,
I do not like you many ways,
And I could do for many days
Without a soft-boiled egg.

Russell Hoban

Here We Go Round the Mulberry Bush

Here we go round the mulberry bush,
The mulberry bush, the mulberry bush,
Here we go round the mulberry bush,
On a cold and frosty morning.

This is the way we wash our hands,
Wash our hands, wash our hands,
This is the way we wash our hands,
On a cold and frosty morning.

This is the way we wash our clothes,
Wash our clothes, wash our clothes,
This is the way we wash our clothes,
On a cold and frosty morning.

Anon.

Skyscraper, Skyscraper

Poems about Town

Busy Day

Pop in

pop out

pop over the road

pop out for a walk

pop in for a talk

pop down to the shop

can't stop

got to pop

got to pop?

pop where?

pop what?

well

I've got to

pop round

pop up

pop in to town

pop out and see

pop in for tea

pop down to the shop

can't stop

got to pop

got to pop?

pop where?

pop what?

well

I've got to

pop in

pop out

pop over the road

pop out for a walk

pop in for a talk . . .

Michael Rosen

Oranges and Lemons

Gay go up and gay go down,
To ring the bells of London town.

Oranges and lemons,
Say the bells of St Clement's.

Brickbats and tiles,
Say the bells of St Giles'.

Halfpence and farthings,
Say the bells of St Martin's.

Pancakes and fritters,
Say the bells of St Peter's.

Two sticks and an apple,
Say the bells at Whitechapel.

Old Father Baldpate,
Say the slow bells at Aldgate.

You owe me ten shillings,
Say the bells at St Helen's.

Pokers and tongs,
Say the bells at St John's.

Kettles and pans,
Say the bells at St Ann's.

When will you pay me,
Say the bells at Old Bailey.

When I grow rich,
Say the bells at Shoreditch.

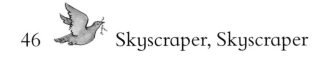

Pray when will that be?
Say the bells of Stepney.

I am sure I don't know,
Says the great bell at Bow.

Here comes a candle to light you to bed,
And here comes a chopper to chop off your head.
Last, last, last, last, last man's head.

Anon.

Cobbler, Cobbler

Cobbler, cobbler, mend my shoe.
Get it done by half-past two;
Stitch it up and stitch it down,
And then I'll give you half a crown.

Anon.

The Postman

Rat-a-tat-tat, Rat-a-tat-tat,
    Rat-a-tat-tat tattoo!
That's the way the Postman goes,
    Rat-a-tat-tat tattoo!
Every morning at half-past eight
You hear a bang at the garden gate,
And Rat-a-tat-tat, Rat-a-tat-tat,
    Rat-a-tat-tat tattoo!

Clive Sansom

Skyscrapers

Do skyscrapers ever grow tired
　　Of holding themselves up high?
Do they ever shiver on frosty nights
　　With their tops against the sky?
Do they feel lonely sometimes,
　　Because they have grown so tall?
Do they ever wish they could just lie down
　　And never get up at all?

Rachel Field

Skyscraper

Skyscraper, skyscraper,
Scrape me some sky:
Tickle the sun
While the stars go by.

Tickle the stars
While the sun's climbing high,
Then skyscraper, skyscraper,
Scrape me some sky.

Dennis Lee

Girls and Boys Come Out to Play

Girls and boys come out to play,
The moon doth shine as bright as day;
Leave your supper and leave your sleep,
And come with your playfellows in the street,
Come with a whoop and come with a call.
Come with a goodwill or not at all.
Up the ladder and down the wall,
A halfpenny roll will serve us all.
You find milk and I'll find flour,
And we'll make a pudding in half an hour.

Anon.

The Pickety Fence

The pickety fence
The pickety fence
Give it a lick it's
The pickety fence
Give it a lick it's
A clickety fence
Give it a lick it's
A lickety fence
Give it a lick
Give it a lick
Give it a lick
With a rickety stick
Pickety
Pickety
Pickety
Pick

David McCord

Mr Brown

Mr Brown
Goes up and down,
And round and round,
And round the town;
Up and down,
Round and round,
Up and down
And round the town.

Rodney Bennett

Old John Muddlecombe

Old John Muddlecombe
   Lost his cap,
He couldn't find it anywhere,
   The poor old chap.
He walked down the High Street,
   And everybody said,
"Silly John Muddlecombe,
   You've got it on your head!"

Anon.

Five Brave Firefighters

Five brave firefighters, standing in a row.
"ONE, TWO, THREE, FOUR, FIVE," they go.
The alarm goes BRIIIING!
They all give a shout,
And jump up on the engine
To put the fire out.

Anon.

Fire! Fire!

"Fire! Fire!" said Mrs Dyer;
"Where? Where?" said Mrs Dare;
"Up the town," said Mrs Brown;
"Any damage?" said Mrs Gamage;
"None at all," said Mrs Hall.

Anon.

Tall Shop in the Town

Tall shop in the town,
Lifts moving up and down.
Doors swinging round about,
People walking in and out.

Anon.

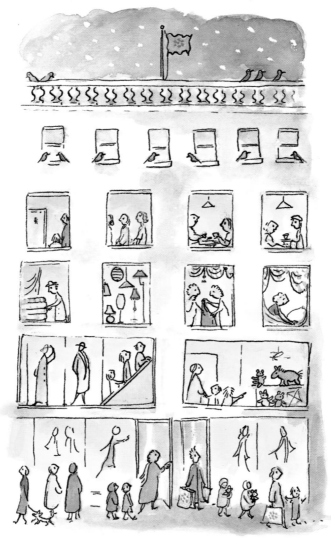

Mrs Mason Bought a Basin

Mrs Mason bought a basin.
Mrs Tyson said, "What a nice 'un."
"What did it cost?" said Mrs Frost.
"Half a crown," said Mrs Brown.
"Did it indeed!" said Mrs Reed.
"It did for certain," said Mrs Burton.
    Then Mrs Nix, up to her tricks,
    Threw the basin on the bricks.

Anon.

Down by the Station

Down by the station
Early in the morning,
See the little puffer trains
All in a row.
See the engine driver
Turn the little handle.
Chug-chug,
Toot-toot,
Off we go.

Anon.

Down the Stream
the Swans All Glide

Down the stream the swans all glide;
It's quite the cheapest way to ride.
Their legs get wet,
Their tummies wetter:
I think after all
The bus is better.

Spike Milligan

Mrs Peck-Pigeon

Mrs Peck-Pigeon
Is picking for bread,
Bob–bob–bob
Goes her little round head.
Tame as a pussy-cat
In the street,
Step–step–step
Go her little red feet.
With her little red feet
And her little round head,
Mrs Peck-Pigeon
Goes picking for bread.

Eleanor Farjeon

Squelching
in My Shoes

Countryside Poems

A Swamp Romp

Clomp Thump
Swamp Lump
Plodding in the Ooze,
Belly Shiver
Jelly Quiver
Squelching in my shoes.

Clomp Thump
Romp Jump
Mulching all the Mud,
Boot Trudge
Foot Sludge
Thud! Thud! Thud!

Doug MacLeod

Squishy Words
(to be said when wet)

SQUIFF

SQUIDGE

SQUAMOUS

SQUINNY

SQUELCH

SQUASH

SQUEEGEE

SQUIRT

SQUAB

Alastair Reid

Ducks' Ditty

All along the backwater,
Through the rushes tall,
Ducks are a-dabbling,
Up tails all!

Ducks' tails, drakes' tails,
Yellow feet a-quiver,
Yellow bills all out of sight
Busy in the river!

Slushy green undergrowth
Where the roach swim—
Here we keep our larder,
Cool and full and dim!

Every one for what he likes!
We like to be
Heads down, tails up,
Dabbling free!

High in the blue above
Swifts whirl and call—
We are down a-dabbling
Up tails all!

Kenneth Grahame

Hurt No Living Thing

 Hurt no living thing:
    Ladybird, nor butterfly,
Nor moth with dusty wing,
    Nor cricket chirping cheerily,
Nor grasshopper so light of leap,
    Nor dancing gnat, nor beetle fat,
Nor harmless worms that creep.

Christina Rossetti

Whisky Frisky

Whisky frisky,
Hipperty hop,
Up he goes
To the tree top!

Whirly, twirly,
Round and round,
Down he scampers
To the ground.

Furly, curly,
What a tail,
Tall as a feather,
Broad as a sail.

Where's his supper?
In the shell.
Snappy, cracky,
Out it fell.

Anon.

To a Squirrel at Kyle-Na-No

Come play with me;
Why should you run
Through the shaking tree
As though I'd a gun
To strike you dead?
When all I would do
Is to scratch your head
And let you go.

W. B. Yeats

The Ferryman

"Ferry me across the water,
        Do, boatman, do."
"If you've a penny in your purse
        I'll ferry you."

"I have a penny in my purse,
        And my eyes are blue;
So ferry me across the water,
        Do, boatman, do."

"Step into my ferry-boat,
        Be they black or blue,
And for the penny in your purse
        I'll ferry you."

Christina Rossetti

Juniper, Juniper

Juniper, Juniper,
    Green in the snow;
Sweetly you smell
    And prickly you grow.

Juniper, Juniper,
    Blue in the fall:
Give me some berries,
    Prickles and all.

Anon.

Five Little Owls

Five little owls in an old elm-tree,
Fluffy and puffy as owls could be,
Blinking and winking with big round eyes
At the big round moon that hung in the skies:
As I passed beneath, I could hear one say,
"There'll be mouse for supper, there will, to-day!"
Then all of them hooted, "Tu-whit, Tu-whoo!
Yes, mouse for supper, Hoo hoo, Hoo hoo!"

Anon.

Owl

A wise old owl sat in an oak,
The more he heard the less he spoke;
The less he spoke the more he heard.
Why aren't we all like that wise old bird?

Anon.

Tree House

A tree house, a free house,
A secret you and me house,
A high up in the leafy branches
Cozy as can be house.

A street house, a neat house,
Be sure and wipe your feet house
Is not my kind of house at all—
Let's go live in a tree house.

Shel Silverstein

What is Pink?

What is pink? a rose is pink
By the fountain's brink.
What is red? a poppy's red
In its barley bed.

What is blue? the sky is blue
Where the clouds float thro'.
What is white? a swan is white
Sailing in the light.

What is yellow? pears are yellow,
Rich and ripe and mellow.
What is green? the grass is green,
With small flowers between.
What is violet? clouds are violet
In the summer twilight.
What is orange? why, an orange,
Just an orange!

Christina Rossetti

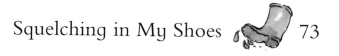

The Rainbow

Boats sail on the rivers,
    And ships sail on the seas;
But clouds that sail across the sky
    Are prettier far than these.

There are bridges on the rivers,
    As pretty as you please;
But the bow that bridges heaven,
    And overtops the trees,
And builds a road from earth to sky,
    Is prettier far than these.

Christina Rossetti

Toadstools

It's not a bit windy,
   It's not a bit wet,
The sky is as sunny
   As summer, and yet
Little umbrellas are
   Everywhere spread,
Pink ones, and brown ones,
   And orange, and red.

I can't see the folks
Who are hidden below;
I've peeped, and I've peeped
Round the edges, but no!
They hold their umbrellas
So tight and so close
That nothing shows under,
Not even a nose!

Elizabeth Fleming

Froggie, Froggie

Froggie, froggie.
Hoppity-hop!
When you get to the sea
You do not stop.
Plop!

Anon.

The Three Foxes

Once upon a time there were
    three little foxes
Who didn't wear stockings,
    and they didn't wear sockses,
But they all had handkerchiefs
    to blow their noses,
And they kept their handkerchiefs
    in cardboard boxes.

They lived in the forest
    in three little houses,
And they didn't wear coats,
    and they didn't wear trousies.
They ran through the woods
    on their little bare tootsies,

And they played "Touch last"
    with a family of mouses.

They didn't go shopping
   in the High Street shopses,
But caught what they wanted
   in the woods and copses.
They all went fishing,
   and they caught three wormses,
They went out hunting,
   and they caught three wopses.

They went to a Fair,
    and they all won prizes—
Three plum-puddingses
    and three mince-pieses.
They rode on elephants
    and swang on swingses,
And hit three coco-nuts
    at coco-nut shieses.

That's all that I know of
    the three little foxes
Who kept their handkerchiefs
    in cardboard boxes.
But they didn't wear coats
    and they didn't wear trousies.
And they didn't wear stockings
    and they didn't wear sockses.

A. A. Milne

Look out Stomach, Here it Comes!

Poems about Food

Sugarcake Bubble

Sugarcake, Sugarcake
    Bubbling in a pot
Bubble, Bubble Sugarcake
    Bubble thick and hot

Sugarcake, Sugarcake
    Spice and coconut
Sweet and sticky
    Brown and gooey

I could eat the lot.

Grace Nichols

Jelly on the Plate

Jelly on the plate,
Jelly on the plate.
Wibble, wobble,
Wibble, wobble,
Jelly on the plate.

Anon.

Polly Put the Kettle On

Polly put the kettle on,
Polly put the kettle on,
Polly put the kettle on,
    We'll all have tea.

Sukey take it off again,
Sukey take it off again,
Sukey take it off again,
    They've all gone away.

Blow the fire and make the toast,
Put the muffins on to roast,
Who is going to eat the most?
    We'll all have tea.

Anon.

Wash the Dishes

Wash the dishes,
Wipe the dishes,
Ring the bell for tea;
Three good wishes,
Three good kisses,
I will give to thee.

Anon.

Peanut Butter and Jelly

First you take the dough and knead it, knead it.

Peanut butter, peanut butter, jelly, jelly.

Pop it in the oven and bake it, bake it.

Peanut butter, peanut butter, jelly, jelly.

Then you take a knife and slice it, slice it.

Peanut butter, peanut butter, jelly, jelly.

Then you take the peanuts and crack them,
    crack them.

Peanut butter, peanut butter, jelly, jelly.

Put them on the floor and mash them,
    mash them.

Peanut butter, peanut butter, jelly, jelly.

Then you take a knife and spread it, spread it.

Peanut butter, peanut butter, jelly, jelly.

Next you take some grapes and squash them,
    squash them.

Peanut butter, peanut butter, jelly, jelly.

Glop it on the bread and smear it, smear it.

Peanut butter, peanut butter, jelly, jelly.

Then you take the sandwich and eat it, eat it.

Peanut butter, peanut butter, jelly, jelly.

Anon.

The Pancake

Mix a pancake,
Stir a pancake,
Pop it in the pan;

Fry the pancake,
Toss the pancake,—
Catch it if you can.

Christina Rossetti

Hot Cross Buns

Hot cross buns! Hot cross buns!
One a penny, two a penny,
Hot cross buns!
If your daughters do not like them
Give them to your sons;
One a penny, two a penny,
Hot cross buns!

Anon.

An Egg for Easter

I want an egg for Easter,
A browny egg for Easter;
I want an egg for Easter,
So I'll tell my browny hen.
    I'll take her corn and water,
    And show her what I've brought her,
    And she'll lay my egg for Easter,
    Inside her little pen.

Irene F. Pawsey

Through the Teeth

Through the teeth
Past the gums
Look out, stomach
Here it comes!

Anon.

Oodles of Noodles

I love noodles. Give me oodles.
Make a mound up to the sun.
Noodles are my favourite foodles.
I eat noodles by the ton.

Lucia and James L. Hymes, Jr.

Bananas and Cream

Bananas and cream,
Bananas and cream:
All we could say was
Bananas and cream.

We couldn't say fruit,
We wouldn't say cow,
We didn't say sugar—
We don't say it now.

Bananas and cream,
Bananas and cream,
All we could shout was
Bananas and cream.

We didn't say why,
We didn't say how;
We forgot it was fruit,
We forgot the old cow;
We *never* said sugar,
We only said *WOW!*

Bananas and cream,
Bananas and cream;
All that we want is
Bananas and cream!

We didn't say dish,
We didn't say spoon;
We said not tomorrow,
But *NOW* and *HOW SOON!*

Bananas and cream,
Bananas and cream?
We yelled for bananas,
Bananas and scream!

David McCord

When Jacky's a Good Boy

When Jacky's a good boy,
He shall have cakes and custard;
But when he does nothing but cry,
He shall have nothing but mustard.

Anon.

Little Jack Horner

Little Jack Horner
Sat in the corner,
Eating a Christmas pie;
He put in his thumb,
And pulled out a plum,
And said, What a good boy am I!

Anon.

Pease Porridge

Pease porridge hot,
    pease porridge cold,
Pease porridge in the pot,
    nine days old.
Some like it hot,
    some like it cold,
Some like it in the pot,
    nine days old.

Anon.

Yellow Butter

Yellow butter purple jelly red jam black bread

Spread it thick
Say it quick

Yellow butter purple jelly red jam black bread

Spread it thicker
Say it quicker

Yellow butter purple jelly red jam black bread

Now repeat it
While you eat it

Yellow butter purple jelly red jam black bread

Don't talk
With your mouth full!

Mary Ann Hoberman

Toaster Time

Tick tick tick tick tick tick tick
Toast up a sandwich quick quick quick
Hamwich
Jamwich
Lick lick lick!

Tick tick tick tick tick tick—stop!
　　POP!

Eve Merriam

Simple Simon

Simple Simon met a pieman
    Going to the fair;
Says Simple Simon to the pieman,
    Let me taste your ware.

Says the pieman to Simple Simon,
    Show me first your penny;
Says Simple Simon to the pieman,
    Indeed I have not any.

Anon.

Pussy Cat Ate the Dumplings

Pussy cat ate the dumplings,
Pussy cat ate the dumplings;
Mamma stood by, and cried, Oh, fie!
Why did you eat the dumplings?

Anon.

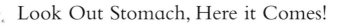

Ice Lolly

Red rocket
on a stick.
If it shines,
lick it quick.

Round the edges,
on the top,
round the bottom,
do not stop.

Suck the lolly,
lick your lips.
Lick the sides
as it drips

off the stick—
quick, quick,
lick, lick—
Red rocket
on a stick.

Pie Corbett

"Purr," says the Cat

Poems for Pets and Friends

The Furry Ones

I like—
the furry ones—
the waggy ones
the purry ones
the hoppy ones
that hurry,

The glossy ones
the saucy ones
the sleepy ones
the leapy ones
the mousy ones
that scurry,

The snuggly ones
the huggly ones
the never, never
ugly ones . . .
all soft
and warm
and furry.

Aileen Fisher

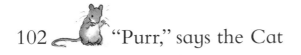

Old Mother Hubbard

Old Mother Hubbard,
She went to the cupboard
To fetch her poor dog a bone,
But when she got there,
The cupboard was bare,
And so the poor dog had none.

Anon.

My Puppy

It's funny
my puppy
knows just how I feel.

When I'm happy
he's yappy
and squirms like an eel.

When I'm grumpy
he's slumpy
and stays at my heel.

It's funny
my puppy
knows such a great deal.

Aileen Fisher

Nipping Pussy's Feet in Fun
(This is Not Kind)

Oh Mr Pussy-Cat

My, you are sweet!

How do you get about so much

On those tiny feet?

Nip, nip, miaou, miaou,

Tiny little feet,

Nip, nip, pussy-cat

My, you are sweet!

Stevie Smith

Cat Asks Mouse Out
(But Then Neither is This)

Mrs Mouse

Come out of your house

It is a fine sunny day

And I am waiting to play.

Bring the little ones too

And we can run to and fro.

Stevie Smith

Mice

I think mice
Are rather nice.

Their tails are long,
Their faces small,
They haven't any
Chins at all.
Their ears are pink,
Their teeth are white,
They run about
The house at night.
They nibble things
They shouldn't touch
And no one seems
To like them much.

But I think mice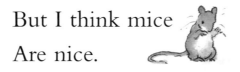
Are nice.

Rose Fyleman

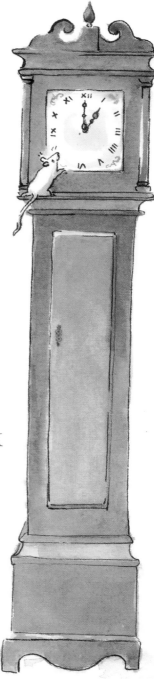

Hickory, Dickory, Dock

Hickory, dickory, dock,
The mouse ran up the clock.
The clock struck one,
The mouse ran down,
Hickory, dickory, dock.

Anon.

I had a Little Horse

I had a little horse,

His name was Dappled Grey.

His head was made of gingerbread,

His tail was made of hay.

He could amble, he could trot,

He could carry the mustard pot,

He could amble, he could trot,

Through the old Town of Windsor.

Anon.

Mary's Lamb

(extract)

Mary had a little lamb,

Its fleece was white as snow,

And everywhere that Mary went

The lamb was sure to go;

He followed her to school one day—

That was against the rule,

It made the children laugh and play

To see a lamb at school.

Sarah Josepha Hale

Choosing Their Names

Our old cat has kittens three—
What do you think their names should be?

One is tabby with emerald eyes,
    And a tail that's long and slender,
And into a temper she quickly flies
    If you ever by chance offend her.
        I think we shall call her this—
        I think we shall call her that—
Now, don't you think that Pepperpot
        Is a nice name for a cat?

One is black with a frill of white,
    And her feet are all white fur,
If you stroke her she carries her tail upright
    And quickly begins to purr.
        I think we shall call her this—
        I think we shall call her that—
Now, don't you think that Sootikin
        Is a nice name for a cat?

One is a tortoiseshell yellow and black,
With plenty of white about him;
If you tease him, at once he sets up his back,
He's a quarrelsome one, ne'er doubt him.
I think we shall call him this—
I think we shall call him that—
Now, don't you think that Scratchaway
Is a nice name for a cat?

Our old cat has kittens three
And I fancy these their names will be:
Pepperpot, Sootikin, Scratchaway—there!
Were ever kittens with these to compare?
And we call the old mother—
Now, what do you think?—
Tabitha Longclaws Tiddley Wink.

Thomas Hood

Once I Saw a Little Bird

Once I saw a little bird
    going hop, hop, hop.
So I cried, "Little bird,
    will you stop, stop, stop?"
And was going to the window
    to say, "How do you do?"
When he shook his little tail
    and away he flew.

Anon.

My Parakeet

Anyone see my parakeet, Skeet?

He's small and neat,

He's really sweet,

With his pick-pick beak,

And his turn-back feet.

Skeet, Skeet, I wouldn't tell a lie

You are the green-pearl of my eye.

Grace Nichols

Oh Where, Oh Where?

Oh where, oh where has my little dog gone?
Oh where, oh where can he be?
With his ears cut short and his tail cut long,
Oh where, oh where is he?

Anon.

Maggie

There was a small maiden named Maggie,
Whose dog was enormous and shaggy;
    The front end of him
    Looked vicious and grim—
But the tail end was friendly and waggy.

Anon.

Dame Trot and Her Cat

Dame Trot and her cat
Sat down for to chat;
The Dame sat on this side,
And Puss sat on that.

"Puss," says the Dame,
"Can you catch a rat,
Or a mouse in the dark?"
"Purr," says the cat.

Anon.

My Cat

My cat
got fatter
and fatter.
I didn't know
what was the matter.
Then,
know what she did?
She went into the cupboard
and hid.

She was fat when she went in,
but she came out
thin.
I had a peep.
Know what I saw?
Little kittens
all in a heap
—1—2—3—4.

My cat's great.

Nigel Gray

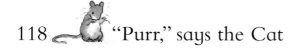

The Little Turtle
(A recitation for Martha
Wakefield, three years old)

There was a little turtle.
He lived in a box.
He swam in a puddle.
He climbed on the rocks.

He snapped at a mosquito.
He snapped at a flea.
He snapped at a minnow.
And he snapped at me.

He caught the mosquito.
He caught the flea.
He caught the minnow.
But he didn't catch me.

Vachel Lindsay

The Squirrel

The winds they did blow,
    The leaves they did wag;
Along came a beggar boy
    And put me in his bag.
He took me to London;
    A lady did me buy,
And put me in a silver cage,
    And hung me up on high;
With apples by the fire,
    And hazelnuts to crack,
Besides a little feather bed
    To rest my tiny back.

Anon.

Cow

The Cow comes home swinging
Her udder and singing:

"The dirt O the dirt
It does me no hurt.

And a good splash of muck
Is a blessing of luck.

O I splosh through the mud
But the breath of my cud

Is sweeter than silk.
O I splush through manure

But my heart stays pure
As a pitcher of milk."

Ted Hughes

Babies
are Funny

Poems about Families

Water Everywhere

There's water on the ceiling,
And water on the wall,
There's water in the bedroom,
And water in the hall,
There's water on the landing,
And water on the stair,
Whenever Daddy takes a bath
There's water everywhere.

Valerie Bloom

Up to the Ceiling

Daddy lifts me
up to the ceiling.
Daddy swings me
down to the floor.
Daddy! Daddy!
More! More! MORE!
Up to the ceiling,
down to the floor.

Charles Thomson

My Folks

Dad is the funniest,
Mum is the best,
Lucy is my helper,
and Daniel is a pest.

Heidi Fish (aged 7)

Brother

I had a little brother
And I brought him to my mother
And I said I want another
Little brother for a change.

But she said don't be a bother
So I took him to my father
And I said this little bother
Of a brother's very strange.

But he said one little brother
Is exactly like another
And every little brother
Misbehaves a bit he said.

So I took the little bother
From my mother and my father
And I put the little bother
Of a brother back to bed.

Mary Ann Hoberman

Little Arabella Miller

Little Arabella Miller
Found a woolly caterpillar.
First it crawled upon her mother
Then upon her baby brother.
All said, "Arabella Miller,
Take away that caterpillar!"

Anon.

There was a Little Girl

There was a little girl
Who had a little curl
Right in the middle of her forehead.
When she was good
She was very, very good,
But when she was bad she was horrid.

Henry Wadsworth Longfellow (attrib.)

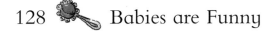

There was an Old Woman who Lived in a Shoe

There was an old woman
    who lived in a shoe,
She had so many children
    she didn't know what to do;
She gave them some broth
    without any bread;
She whipped them all soundly
    and put them to bed.

Anon.

Ask Mummy Ask Daddy

When I ask Daddy
Daddy says ask Mummy

When I ask Mummy
Mummy says ask Daddy.
I don't know where to go.

Better ask my teddy
he never says no.

John Agard

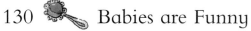

Daddy

Me so small
And you so tall,
Why can't you get the stars
From the sky after all?

Vyanne Samuels

Mocking Bird

Hush, little baby, don't say a word,
Papa's going to buy you a mocking bird.

If the mocking bird won't sing,
Papa's going to buy you a diamond ring.

If the diamond ring turns to brass,
Papa's going to buy you a looking-glass.

If the looking-glass gets broke,
Papa's going to buy you a billy-goat.

If that billy-goat runs away,
Papa's going to buy you another today.

Anon.

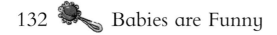

Salty Sea

Salty sandcastle,
Salty sea,
Salty footprints,
Salty me.

Carl Saville (aged 5)

To the Sea!

Who'll be first?
Shoes off,
in a row,
four legs fast,
two legs slow—
Ready now?
Off we go!
Tip-toe,
dip-a-toe,
heel and toe—
Yes or no?
Cold as snow!
All at once,
in we go!
One,
    two,
        three,
            SPLASH!

Judith Nicholls

Hugs

I've three special hugs for you, Granny,
Hug one, hug two, and hug three.
This hug's from rabbit,
This hug's from hippo,
And this snuggly huggle's from me.

Michelle Magorian

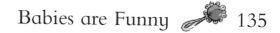

Squeezes

We love to squeeze bananas,
We love to squeeze ripe plums,
And when they are feeling sad
We love to squeeze our mums.

Brian Patten

Little

I am the sister of him
And he is my brother.
He is too little for us
To talk to each other.

So every morning I show him
My doll and my book;
But every morning he still is
Too little to look.

Dorothy Aldis

Babies

Babies are funny.
They don't speak a lot.
They can't drink from cups
Or sit on a pot.

They like to grip fingers.
They like milk from mummies.
They like having raspberries
Blown on their tummies.

They like being cuddled
And kissed on the head.
But they don't say a lot,
They just dribble instead.

Michelle Magorian

What Someone Said
When He Was Spanked
On the Day Before His Birthday

Some day
I may
Pack my bag and run away.
Some day
I may.
—But not today.

Some night
I might
Slip away in the moonlight.
I might.
Some night.
—But not tonight.

Some night.

Some day.

I might.

I may.

—But right now I think I'll stay.

John Ciardi

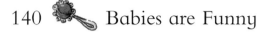

Noise

Billy is blowing his trumpet;
Bertie is banging a tin;
Betty is crying for Mummy
And Bob has pricked Ben with a pin.
Baby is crying out loudly;
He's out on the lawn in his pram.
I am the only one silent
And I've eaten all of the jam.

Anon.

Potty

Don't put that potty on your head, Tim.
Don't put that potty on your head.
 It's not very clean
 And you don't know where it's been,
So don't put that potty on your head.

Colin McNaughton

Dance to your Daddy

Dance to your daddy,
My little babby,
Dance to your daddy,
My little lamb;

You shall have a fishy
In a little dishy,
You shall have a fishy
When the boat comes in.

Baby shall have an apple,
Baby shall have a plum,
Baby shall have a rattle
When Daddy comes home.

Anon.

One, Two, Buckle My Shoe

Counting Poems

One, Two, Buckle My Shoe

One, two,
Buckle my shoe;

Three, four,
Knock at the door;

Five, six,
Pick up sticks;

Seven, eight,
Lay them straight;

Nine, ten,
A big fat hen;

Eleven, twelve,
Dig and delve;

Thirteen, fourteen,
Maids a-courting;

Fifteen, sixteen,
Maids in the kitchen;

Seventeen, eighteen,
Maids in waiting;

Nineteen, twenty,
My plate's empty.

Anon.

Mosquito One Mosquito Two

Mosquito one
mosquito two
mosquito jump
in de old man shoe.

Anon.

Fortunes

One for sorrow, two for joy,
Three for a kiss and four for a boy,
Five for silver, six for gold,
Seven for a secret never to be told,
Eight for a letter over the sea,
Nine for a lover as true as can be.

Anon.

Chook, Chook, Chook

Chook, chook, chook, chook, chook,
    Good morning, Mrs Hen.
How many chickens have you got?
    Madam, I've got ten.
Four of them are yellow,
    And four of them are brown,
And two of them are speckled red,
    The nicest in the town.

Anon.

Old Noah's Ark

Old Noah once he built an ark,
And patched it up with hickory bark.
He anchored it to a great big rock,
And then he began to load his stock.
The animals went in one by one,
The elephant chewing a carroway bun.
The animals went in two by two,
The crocodile and the kangaroo.

The animals went in three by three,
The tall giraffe and the tiny flea.
The animals went in four by four,
The hippopotamus stuck in the door.
The animals went in five by five,
The bees mistook the bear for a hive.
The animals went in six by six,
The monkey was up to his usual tricks.

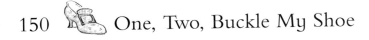

The animals went in seven by seven,

Said the ant to the elephant, "Who're ye shov'n?"

The animals went in eight by eight,

Some were early and some were late.

The animals went in nine by nine,

They all formed fours and marched in a line.

The animals went in ten by ten,

If you want any more, you can read it again.

Anon.

One, Two, Three, Four

One, two, three, four,
Mary at the cottage door,
Five, six, seven, eight,
Eating cherries off a plate.

Anon.

One, Two, Three, Four, Five

One, two, three, four, five,
Once I caught a fish alive,
Six, seven, eight, nine, ten,
Then I let it go again.
Why did you let it go?
Because it bit my finger so.
Which finger did it bite?
This little finger on the right.

Anon.

Ten Fat Sausages

*Pretend each finger is a sausage and clap when the sausages
pop and bang.*

Ten fat sausages sitting in the pan;
One went, "Pop!" and another went, "Bang!"

Eight fat sausages sitting in the pan;
One went, "Pop!" and another went, "Bang!"

Six fat sausages sitting in the pan;
One went, "Pop!" and another went, "Bang!"

Four fat sausages sitting in the pan;
One went, "Pop!" and another went, "Bang!"

Two fat sausages sitting in the pan;
One went, "Pop!" and another went, "Bang!"

No more sausages sitting in the pan!

Anon.

Five Little Peas

Five little peas in a pea-pod pressed,

Make one of your hands into a fist.

One grew, two grew and so did all the rest.

Raise your fingers slowly, one at a time.

They grew and grew and did not stop,

Stretch your fingers wide.

Until one day the pod went POP!

Clap loudly as you say "POP".

Anon.

Five Little Pussy Cats

Five little pussy cats playing near the door;
One ran and hid inside
And then there were four.

Four little pussy cats underneath a tree;
One heard a dog bark
And then there were three.

Three little pussy cats thinking what to do;
One saw a little bird
And then there were two.

Two little pussy cats sitting in the sun;
One ran to catch his tail
And then there was one.

One little pussy cat looking for some fun;
He saw a butterfly—
And then there was none.

Anon.

I Love Sixpence

I love sixpence, jolly little sixpence,
    I love sixpence better than my life;
I spent a penny of it, I lent a penny of it,
    And I took fourpence home to my wife.

Oh, my little fourpence, jolly little fourpence,
    I love fourpence better than my life;
I spent a penny of it, I lent a penny of it,
    And I took twopence home to my wife.

Oh, my little twopence, jolly little twopence,
    I love twopence better than my life;
I spent a penny of it, I lent a penny of it,
    And I took nothing home to my wife.

Oh, my little nothing, jolly little nothing,
    What will nothing buy for my wife?
I have nothing, I spend nothing,
    I love nothing better than my wife.

Anon.

Mudpie Stew

Garden Poems

Mary, Mary, Quite Contrary

Mary, Mary, quite contrary,
    How does your garden grow?
With silver bells and cockle shells,
    And pretty maids all in a row.

Anon.

A Garden

If I should have a garden
I know how it would be,
There'd be daisies and buttercups
And an apple tree.

A dog would chase a ball there,
A bird would sit and sing,
And a little cat would play with
A little piece of string.

And in the very middle
I'd only have to stand
For ladybirds and butterflies
To settle on my hand.

Leila Berg

The Caterpillar

Brown and furry
Caterpillar in a hurry,
Take your walk
To the shady leaf, or stalk,
Or what not,
Which may be the chosen spot.
No toad spy you,
Hovering bird of prey pass by you;
Spin and die,
To live again a butterfly.

Christina Rossetti

Only My Opinion

Is a caterpillar ticklish?
Well, it's always my belief
That he giggles, as he wiggles
Across a hairy leaf.

Monica Shannon

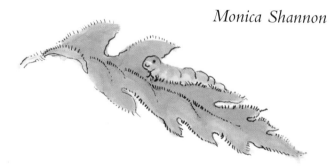

Today I Saw a Little Worm

Today I saw a little worm
Wriggling on his belly.
Perhaps he'd like to come inside
And see what's on the Telly.

Spike Milligan

Little Brown Seed

Little brown seed, round and sound,
Here I put you in the ground.

You can sleep a week or two,
Then—I'll tell you what to do:

You must grow some downward roots,
Then some tiny upward shoots.

From those green shoots' folded sheaves
Soon must come some healthy leaves.

When the leaves have time to grow,
Next a bunch of buds must show.

Last of all, the buds must spread
Into blossoms white or red.

There, Seed! I've done my best.
Please to grow and do the rest.

Rodney Bennett

A Spike of Green

When I went out
The sun was hot,
It shone upon
My flower pot.

And there I saw
A spike of green
That no one else
Had ever seen!

On other days
The things I see
Are mostly old
Except for me.

But this green spike
So new and small
Had never yet
Been seen at all!

Barbara Baker

Spin Me a Web, Spider

Spin me a web, spider,
Across the window-pane
For I shall never break it
And make you start again.

Cast your net of silver
As soon as it is spun,
And hang it with the morning dew
That glitters in the sun.

It's strung with pearls and diamonds,
The finest ever seen,
Fit for any royal King
Or any royal Queen.

Would you, could you, bring it down
In the dust to lie?
Any day of the week, my dear,
Said the nimble fly.

Charles Causley

Little Miss Muffet

Little Miss Muffet
Sat on a tuffet,
Eating her curds and whey;
There came a big spider,
Who sat down beside her
And frightened Miss Muffet away.

Anon.

Little Miss Tuckett

Little Miss Tuckett
Sat on a bucket,
Eating some peaches and cream;
There came a grasshopper,
And tried hard to stop her;
But she said, Go away, or I'll scream.

Anon.

Swinging

Slowly, slowly, swinging low,
Let me see how far I go!
Slowly, slowly, keeping low,
I see where the wild flowers grow!

(Getting quicker):

Quicker, quicker,
Swinging higher,
I can see
A shining spire!
Quicker, quicker,
Swinging higher,
I can see
The sunset's fire!

Faster, faster,
Through the air,
I see almost
Everywhere.
Woods and hills,
And sheep that stare—
And things I never
Knew were there!

(Getting slower):

Slower, slower, now I go,
Swinging, dreaming, getting low;
Slowly, slowly, down I go—
Till I touch the grass below.

Irene Thompson

The Snail

Snail upon the wall,
Have you got at all
Anything to tell
About your shell?

Only this, my child—
When the wind is wild
Or when the sun is hot,
It's all I've got.

John Drinkwater

Mud

Take a bucket of soil.
Some water from a can.
Mix them well
in an old saucepan.
Add a few leaves.
Some flowerpetals too.
And soon you'll have
A Mudpie stew.

Take slugs and snails,
a scattering of sand.
Rub them round
with your muddy hand.
Leave in the sun
a while to bake.
And soon you'll have
A Mudpie cake.

Ann Bonner

What do you Suppose?

What do you suppose?
A bee sat on my nose.
Then what do you think?
He gave me a wink
And said, "I beg your pardon,
I thought you were the garden."

Anon.

The Kitty Ran Up the Tree

The kitty ran up the tree.
The kitty ran up the tree,
Her nose went up
And her toes went up
And the kitty ran up the tree.

Why did she climb the tree?
To see what a kitty could see.
But all she could see
At the top of the tree
Was the tip of the top of the tree—

So—

The kitty came down the tree.
The kitty came down the tree,
Her nose came down
And her toes came down
And the kitty came down the tree.

Dennis Lee

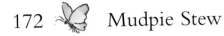

If I were an Apple

If I were an apple
And grew upon a tree,
I think I'd fall down
On a good boy like me.
I wouldn't stay there
Giving nobody joy;
I'd fall down at once
And say, "Eat me, my boy."

Anon.

If You Should Meet a Crocodile

Poems about Wild Animals

Shark

Ever see
a shark
picnic
in the park?

If he offers
you a bun

run.

Roger McGough

If You Ever

If you ever ever ever ever ever
    If you ever ever ever meet a whale
You must never never never never never
    You must never never never touch its tail;
For if you ever ever ever ever ever
    If you ever ever ever touch its tail,
You will never never never never never
    You will never never meet another whale.

Anon.

If You Should Meet a Crocodile

If you should meet a crocodile,
Don't take a stick and poke him;
Ignore the welcome in his smile,
Be careful not to stroke him.
For as he sleeps upon the Nile,
He thinner gets and thinner;
But whene'er you meet a crocodile
He's ready for his dinner.

Anon.

Tiger

I'm a tiger
Striped with fur
Don't come near
Or I might Grrr
Don't come near
Or I might growl
Don't come near
Or I might BITE!

Mary Ann Hoberman

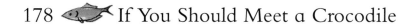

The Eel

I don't mind eels
Except as meals.
And the way they feels.

Ogden Nash

Hippopotamus

The hippopotamus—
how odd—
loves rolling
in the river mud.

It makes him
neither hale nor ruddy,
just lovely
hippopotamuddy.

N. M. Bodecker

Turtles

When turtles hide within their shells
There is no way of knowing
Which is front and which is back
And which way which is going.

John Travers Moore

Little Fish

The tiny fish enjoy themselves
in the sea.
Quick little splinters of life,
their little lives are fun to them
in the sea.

D. H. Lawrence

Ticklish

When is a
stickleback
ticklish?

When it's
tickled
with a
little stick
of liquorice.

Roger McGough

The Elephant

When people call this beast to mind,
  They marvel more and more
At such a little tail behind
  So *large* a trunk before.

Hilaire Belloc

Way Down South

Way down South where bananas grow,
A grasshopper stepped on an elephant's toe.
The elephant said, with tears in his eyes,
"Pick on somebody your own size."

Anon.

Bears

Roly poly polar bears,
Rolling in the snow,
Sliding over icebergs,
In the sea they go:

Splish, splash polar bears,
Splish, splash, splosh!

Growly brown mountain bears,
Climbing on all fours,
Hugging each other
With their big brown paws:

Stump, stomp brown bears,
Stump, stomp, stamp!

Celia Warren

Honey Bear

There was a big bear
Who lived in a cave;
His greatest love
Was honey.
He had twopence a week
Which he never could save,
So he never had
Any money.
I bought him a money box
Red and round,
In which to put
His money.
He saved and saved
Till he got a pound,
　Then spent it all
　On honey.

Elizabeth Lang

Geraldine Giraffe

The
longest
ever
woolly
scarf
was
worn
by
Geraldine
Giraffe.
Around
her
neck
the scarf
she wound,
but still
it trailed
upon
the
ground.

Colin West

Giraffes Don't Huff

Giraffes don't huff or hoot or howl
They never grump, they never growl
They never roar, they never riot,
They eat green leaves
And just keep quiet.

Karla Kuskin

The Kangaroo

Old Jumpety-Bumpety-Hop-and-Go-One
Was lying asleep on his side in the sun.
This old kangaroo, he was whisking the flies
(With his long glossy tail) from his ears
　　and his eyes.
Jumpety-Bumpety-Hop-and-Go-One
Was lying asleep on his side in the sun,
Jumpety-Bumpety-Hop!

Anon.

Penguin

Big flapper
Belly tapper
Big splasher
Fish catcher
Beak snapper.

Rebecca Clark (aged 8)

Dinosauristory

Hocus, pocus,
plodding through the swamp;
I'm a diplodocus,
chomp, chomp, chomp!
Grass for breakfast,
I could eat a tree!
Grass for lunch and dinner
and grass for tea.
I'm a diplodocus
plodding through the swamp,
hocus-rocus pocus,
chomp, chomp, chomp!

Judith Nicholls

If I Were a Queen

Royal Poems

If I were a Queen

If I were a Queen,
    What would I do?
I'd make you King,
    And I'd wait on you.

If I were a King,
    What would I do?
I'd make you Queen,
    For I'd marry you.

Christina Rossetti

Lavender's Blue

Lavender's blue, diddle, diddle,
　　Lavender's green,
When I am king, diddle, diddle,
　　You shall be queen.

Call up your men, diddle, diddle,
　　Set them to work,
Some to the plough, diddle, diddle,
　　Some to the cart.

Some to make hay, diddle, diddle,
　　Some to thresh corn,
Whilst you and I, diddle, diddle,
　　Keep ourselves warm.

Anon.

Pussy Cat, Pussy Cat

Pussy cat, pussy cat,
    where have you been?
I've been to London
    to look at the queen.

Pussy cat, pussy cat,
    what did you there?
I frightened a little mouse
    under her chair.

Anon.

Pumpkin Pumpkin

Pumpkin
Pumpkin
Where have you been?

I been to Hallowe'en
to frighten the queen

Pumpkin
Pumpkin
how did you do it?

With two holes for my eyes
and a light
in me head

I frightened the queen
right under her bed!

John Agard

Humpty Dumpty

Humpty Dumpty sat on a wall,
Humpty Dumpty had a great fall;
    All the king's horses,
    And all the king's men,
Couldn't put Humpty together again.

Anon.

The Lion and the Unicorn

The Lion and the Unicorn
   Were fighting for the crown;
The Lion beat the Unicorn
   All about the town.
Some gave them white bread,
   And some gave them brown,
Some gave them plum cake,
   And sent them out of town.

Anon.

The Queen of Hearts

The Queen of Hearts,
  She made some tarts,
All on a summer's day;
  The Knave of Hearts,
  He stole the tarts,
And took them clean away!

The King of Hearts
  Called for the tarts,
And beat the Knave full sore;
  The Knave of Hearts
  Brought back the tarts,
And vowed he'd steal no more.

Anon.

Hector Protector

Hector Protector was dressed all in green;
Hector Protector was sent to the Queen.
The Queen did not like him,
No more did the King;
So Hector Protector was sent back again.

Anon.

Sing a Song of Sixpence

Sing a song of sixpence,
  A pocket full of rye;
Four and twenty blackbirds,
  Baked in a pie.

When the pie was opened,
The birds began to sing;
Was not that a dainty dish,
To set before the king?

The king was in his counting-house,
Counting out his money;
The queen was in the parlour,
Eating bread and honey.

The maid was in the garden,
Hanging out the clothes,
Along came a blackbird,
And snapped off her nose.

Anon.

I had a Little Nut Tree

I had a little nut tree,
     Nothing would it bear
But a silver nutmeg
     And a golden pear;
The King of Spain's daughter
     Came to visit me,
And all for the sake
     Of my little nut tree.

Anon.

Lilies are White

Lilies are white,
   Rosemary's green;
When you are king,
   I will be queen.

Roses are red,
   Lavender's blue;
If you will have me,
   I will have you.

Anon.

Old King Cole

Old King Cole was a merry old soul,
And a merry old soul was he;
He called for his pipe,
And he called for his bowl,
And he called for his fiddlers three.

Each fiddler he had a fiddle,
And the fiddles went tweedle-dee;
Oh, there's none so rare as can compare
With King Cole and his fiddlers three.

Anon.

How Many Miles to Babylon?

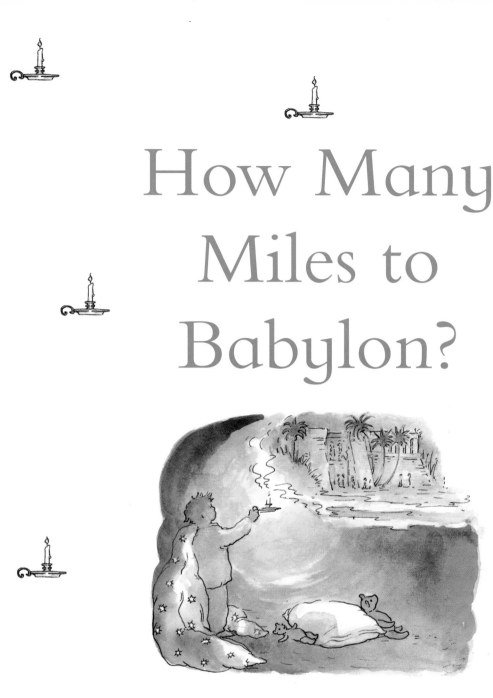

Poems about Journeys

The Owl and the Pussy-Cat

The Owl and the Pussy-cat went to sea
   In a beautiful pea-green boat,
They took some honey, and plenty of money,
   Wrapped up in a five-pound note.
The Owl looked up to the stars above,
   And sang to a small guitar,
"O lovely Pussy! O Pussy, my love,
   What a beautiful Pussy you are,
      You are,
      You are!
   What a beautiful Pussy you are!"

Pussy said to the Owl, "You elegant fowl!
    How charmingly sweet you sing!
O let us be married! too long we have tarried:
    But what shall we do for a ring?"
They sailed away, for a year and a day,
    To the land where the Bong-tree grows
And there in a wood a Piggy-wig stood
    With a ring at the end of his nose,
        His nose,
        His nose,
    With a ring at the end of his nose.

"Dear Pig, are you willing to sell for one shilling
  Your ring?" Said the Piggy, "I will."
So they took it away, and were married next day
  By the Turkey who lives on the hill.
They dined on mince, and slices of quince,
  Which they ate with a runcible spoon;
And hand in hand, on the edge of the sand,
  They danced by the light of the moon,
    The moon,
    The moon,
  They danced by the light of the moon.

Edward Lear

The Grand Old Duke of York

Oh, the grand old Duke of York,
  He had ten thousand men,
He marched them up to the top of the hill,
  And he marched them down again.

And when they were up they were up,
  And when they were down they were down,
And when they were only half way up,
  They were neither up nor down.

Anon.

Ride a Cock-Horse

Ride a cock-horse
   to Banbury Cross,
To see a fine lady
   upon a white horse;
With rings on her fingers
   and bells on her toes,
She shall have music
   wherever she goes.

Anon.

How Many Miles to Babylon?

How many miles to Babylon?
Three score miles and ten.
Can I get there by candle-light?
Yes, and back again.
If your heels are nimble and light,
You may get there by candle-light.

Anon.

Row, Row, Row Your Boat

Row, row, row your boat
Gently down the stream.
Merrily, merrily, merrily, merrily,
Life is but a dream.

Anon.

Needles and Pins

Needles and pins,
Needles and pins,
Sew me a sail
To catch me the wind.

Sew me a sail
Strong as the gale,
Carpenter, bring out your
Hammers and nails.

Hammers and nails,
Hammers and nails,
Build me a boat
To go chasing the whales.

Chasing the whales,
Sailing the blue,
Find me a captain
And sign me a crew.

Captain and crew,
Captain and crew,
Take me, oh take me
To anywhere new.

Shel Silverstein

Brown-River Brown-River

Brown-River
Brown-River
Why do you run
You must be trying
To catch-up with someone?

O I'm on my way
To catch-up with the sea
But however fast I run
There's always more of me
Always more of me.

Grace Nichols

Little Silver Aeroplane

Little silver aeroplane
Up in the sky,
Where are you going to
Flying so high?
Over the mountains
Over the sea
Little silver aeroplane
Please take me.

Anon.

The Holiday Train

Here is the train!
Here is the train!
Let us get in!
Let us get in!

Where shall we sit?
Where shall we sit?
When will it go?
When will it go?

What does it say?
What does it say?
"Let us get on!"
"Let us get on!"

Look at the trees!
Look at the trees!
See all the cows!
See all the cows!

Isn't it fun?
Isn't it fun?
Going along!
Going along!

Hurrying on!
Hurrying on!
Nearly there!
Nearly there!

Look at the sea!
Look at the sea!
See all the ships!
See all the ships!

Here we are!
Here we are!
Out we get!
Out we get

Irene Thompson

Gee up, Neddy

Gee up, Neddy, to the fair,
What shall I buy when I get there?
A ha'penny apple, a penny pear.
Gee up, Neddy, to the fair.

Anon.

To Market, to Market

To market, to market, to buy a fat pig;
Home again, home again, jiggety jig.
To market, to market, to buy a fine hog;
Home again, home again, joggety jog.

To market, to market,
   to buy a plum bun;
Home again, home again,
   market is done.

Anon.

I Saw a Ship A-Sailing

I saw a ship a-sailing,
    A-sailing on the sea,
And oh but it was laden
    With pretty things for me.

There were comfits in the cabin,
    And apples in the hold;
The sails were made of silk,
    And the masts were all of gold.

The four-and-twenty sailors,
    That stood between the decks,
Were four-and-twenty white mice
    With chains about their necks.

The captain was a duck
    With a packet on his back,
And when the ship began to move
    The captain said Quack! Quack!

Anon.

Where go the Boats?

Dark brown is the river,
    Golden is the sand.
It flows along for ever,
    With trees on either hand.

Green leaves a-floating,
    Castles of the foam,
Boats of mine a-boating—
    Where will all come home?

On goes the river
    And out past the mill,
Away down the valley,
    Away down the hill.

Away down the river,
    A hundred miles or more,
Other little children
    Shall bring my boats ashore.

Robert Louis Stevenson

We're Off!

We're off
We're off
We're off in our motor car.
Fifty tigers are after us,
FIFTY TIGERS ARE AFTER US,
FIFTY TIGERS ARE AFTER US
And they don't know where we are.

Traditional
(this version by Katherine Alexander)

Doctor Foster

Doctor Foster
Went to Gloucester
In a shower of rain;
He stepped in a puddle,
Right up to his middle,
And never went there again.

Anon.

From a Railway Carriage

Faster than fairies, faster than witches,
Bridges and houses, hedges and ditches;
And charging along like troops in a battle,
All through the meadows the horses and cattle;
All of the sights of the hill and the plain
Fly as thick as driving rain;
And ever again, in the wink of an eye,
Painted stations whistle by.

Here is a child who clambers and scrambles,
All by himself and gathering brambles;
Here is a tramp who stands and gazes;
And there is the green for stringing the daisies!
Here is a cart run away in the road
Lumping along with man and load;
And here is a mill, and there is a river:
Each a glimpse and gone for ever!

Robert Louis Stevenson

Horsie, Horsie

Horsie, horsie, don't you stop,
Just let your feet go clipetty clop;
Your tail goes swish, and the wheels go round—
Giddy up, you're homeward bound!

Anon.

I Can Tie My Shoelace

Poems about Me

In the Mirror

In the mirror
On the wall,
There's a face
I always see;
Round and pink,
And rather small,
Looking back again
At me.

It is very
Rude to stare,
But she never
Thinks of that,
For her eyes are
Always there;
What can she be
Looking at?

Elizabeth Fleming

Everybody Says

Everybody says
I look just like my mother.
Everybody says
I'm the image of Aunt Bee.
Everybody says
My nose is like my father's
But *I* want to look like *ME*!

Dorothy Aldis

I Speak, I Say, I Talk

Cats purr.

Lions roar.

Owls hoot.

Bears snore.

Crickets creak.

Mice squeak.

Sheep baa.

But I SPEAK!

Monkeys chatter.

Cows moo.

Ducks quack.

Doves coo.

Pigs squeal.

Horses neigh.

Chickens cluck.

But I SAY!

Flies hum.

Dogs growl.

Bats screech.

Coyotes howl.

Frogs croak.

Parrots squawk.

Bees buzz.

But I TALK!

Arnold L. Shapiro

Buttons

Buttons, buttons,
I can do up buttons!
I do all my buttons up
When I go to town.
For I have six buttons,
Big round buttons,
Six buttons on my coat
All coloured brown!

W. Kingdon-Ward

Dufflecoat

It has four toggles made of wood,
it's warm and snug inside the hood—
but I find it very diffle-dufflecult
to do up my navy fiddle-fuddlecoat.

John Rice

Giant

I come up to
My brother's knee.
But that's because
I'm only three.

But when I'm four
I will be able
To see what's on
The kitchen table.

And when I'm five
I know that I
Will be so big
I'll reach the sky.

Clive Webster

Upside Down

It's funny how beetles
and creatures like that
can walk upside down
as well as walk flat.

They crawl on a ceiling
and climb on a wall
without any practice
or trouble at all.

While I have been trying
for a year (maybe more)
and still I can't stand
with my head on the floor.

Aileen Fisher

Blue Wellies, Yellow Wellies

Blue wellies, yellow wellies,
green wellies, red.
You wear yours in puddles—
I wear mine in bed!

Judith Nicholls

New Shoes

My shoes are new and squeaky shoes,
They're very shiny, creaky shoes,
I wish I had my leaky shoes
That Mother threw away.

I liked my old, brown, leaky shoes
Much better than these creaky shoes,
These shiny, creaky, squeaky shoes
I've got to wear today.

Anon.

Who Is It?

Take . . .

    A head, some shoulders, knees, and toes,

    A mouth and eyes that see,

    A pair of legs, two feet, one nose,

    And what you've got is

            ME!

Theresa Heine

The Little Old Lady

That little grey-haired lady
    Is as old as old can be,
Yet once she was a little girl,
    A little girl like me.

She liked to skip instead of walk,
    She wore her hair in curls;
She went to school at nine, and played
    With other little girls.

I wonder if, in years and years,
    Some little girl at play,
Who's very like what I am now,
    Will stop to look my way,

And think: "That grey-haired lady
    Is as old as old can be,
Yet once she was a little girl,
    A little girl like me."

Rodney Bennett

I Won't

I won't, no I won't, no I won't do that.
I don't want to, I don't have to,
No I won't wear that hat.

I hate it, yes I hate it, yes I hate hate hate.
You can't make me, I don't want to,
I don't care if we are late.

Yes I'm naughty, yes I'm naughty,
Yes I know, know, know.
But I won't wear that hat
So it's No! No! No!

Michelle Magorian

Hope

Sometimes when I'm lonely,
Don't know why,
Keep thinkin' I won't be lonely
By and by.

Langston Hughes

I Can Tie My Shoelace

I can tie my shoelace,
I can comb my hair.
I can wash my hands and face,
And dry myself with care.
I can brush my teeth, too,
And button up my frocks;
I can say, "How do you do?"
And put on both my socks.

Anon.

I Can Put My Socks On

I can put my socks on,
I can find my vest,
I can put my pants on—
I can't do the rest.

Tony Bradman

Who Likes Cuddles?

Who likes cuddles?

Me.

Who likes hugs?

Me.

Who likes squeezes?

Me.

Who likes tickles?

Me.

Who likes getting their face stroked?

Me.

Who likes being lifted up high?
Me.
Who likes sitting on laps?
Me.
Who likes being whirled round and round?
Me.
But best of all I like
getting into bed and getting blowy blowy
down my neck behind my ear.
A big warm tickly blow
lovely.

Michael Rosen

Something About Me

There's something about me
That I'm knowing.
There's something about me
That isn't showing.

I'm growing!

Anon.

I'm a Little Teapot

Action Rhymes

This Little Pig

*Starting with the big toe, pretend each of the child's toes
is a little pig. On the last line, tickle under the child's foot.*

This little pig went to market,

This little pig stayed at home,

This little pig had roast beef,

And this little pig had none,

And this little pig went wee-wee-wee
all the way home.

Anon.

Round and Round the Garden

Round and round the garden
Went the teddy bear,

Run your finger round the child's palm.

One step,

Two steps,

"Jump" your fingers up his arm.

Tickly under there!

Tickle him under his arm.

Round and round the haystack,
Went the little mouse,
One step,
Two steps,
In his little house.

Repeat the same actions for the second verse.

Anon.

Ring-a-Ring o' Roses

Children hold hands and skip round in a ring.
On the last line of each verse they all sit down on
the ground.

Ring-a-ring o' roses,

A pocket full of posies.

A-tishoo! A-tishoo!

We all fall down.

Ring-a-ring o' roses,

A pocket full of posies.

One for you, and one for me,

And one for little Moses.

A-tishoo! A-tishoo! We all fall down.

Anon.

Two Little Dicky Birds

Two little dicky birds
Sitting on a wall,

Use your two index fingers to be Peter and Paul.

One named Peter,

Wiggle the finger which is Peter.

One named Paul.

Wiggle the finger which is Paul.

Fly away Peter,

Put the finger which is Peter behind your back.

Fly away Paul;

Put the finger which is Paul behind your back.

Come back Peter,

Come back Paul.

Bring each finger back in front of you.

Anon.

Pat-a-Cake

A clapping rhyme to play with a baby.

Pat-a-cake, pat-a-cake, baker's man,
Bake me a cake as fast as you can;
Pat it and prick it, and mark it with B,
Put it in the oven for Baby and me.

Anon.

See-Saw, Margery Daw

*Swing the child gently back and forth on your lap
in time to the words.*

See-saw, Margery Daw,

Johnny shall have a new master;

He shall have but a penny a day,

Because he can't work any faster.

Anon.

The Wheels on the Bus

Mime the action of the wheels going round, the horn peeping, the mums chattering (you can do this by holding your thumb and four straight fingers to make a beak shape, and opening and closing it), the dads nodding and the kids wriggling.

The wheels on the bus go round and round,
    Round and round,
    Round and round,
The wheels on the bus go round and round,
    Over the city streets.

The horn on the bus goes peep, peep, peep,
    Peep, peep, peep,
    Peep, peep, peep,
The horn on the bus goes peep, peep, peep,
    Over the city streets.

The mums on the bus go chatter, chatter, chatter,
    Chatter, chatter, chatter,
    Chatter, chatter, chatter,
The mums on the bus go chatter, chatter, chatter,
    Over the city streets.

The dads on the bus go nod, nod, nod,
   Nod, nod, nod,
   Nod, nod, nod,
The dads on the bus go nod, nod, nod,
   Over the city streets.

The kids on the bus go wriggle, wriggle, wriggle,
   Wriggle, wriggle, wriggle,
   Wriggle, wriggle, wriggle,
The kids on the bus go wriggle, wriggle, wriggle,
   Over the city streets.

Anon.

Teddy Bear

Do the same actions as teddy!

Teddy bear,
Teddy bear, touch your nose,
Teddy bear,
Teddy bear, touch your toes,
Teddy bear,
Teddy bear, touch the ground,
Teddy bear,
Teddy bear, turn around.

Teddy bear,
Teddy bear, climb the stairs,
Teddy bear,
Teddy bear, say your prayers,
Teddy bear,
Teddy bear, turn off the light,
Teddy bear,
Teddy bear, say good night!

Anon.

The Elephant

An elephant goes like this and that.

Pat your knees.

He's terrible big,

Stretch your arms up high.

And he's terrible fat.

Stretch your arms out wide.

He has no fingers,

Wriggle your fingers.

And he has no toes,

Touch your toes.

But goodness gracious, what a nose!

Make a curling movement away from your nose.

Anon.

Here is the Ostrich

Pretend to be each animal in the poem.

Here is the ostrich straight and tall,
Nodding his head above us all.

Here is the long snake on the ground,
Wriggling on the stones around.

Here are the birds that fly so high,
Spreading their wings across the sky.

Here is the bushrat, furry and small,
Rolling himself into a ball.

Here is the spider scuttling round,
Treading so lightly on the ground.

Here are the children fast asleep,
And here at night the owls do peep.

Anon.

Down in the Grass

Pretend your arm is the snake. You could rest your elbow on a table to do this. Make the snake's head by touching your fingertip with your thumb.

Down in the grass, curled up in a heap,

Lies a big snake, fast asleep.

When he hears the grasses blow,

He moves his body to and fro.

Up and down and in and out,

See him slowly move about!

Now his jaws are open, so—

Snap! He's caught my finger! Oh!

Anon.

Can You Walk on Tip-Toe?

Walk around as the words suggest.

Can you walk on tip-toe
As softly as a cat?
And can you stamp along the road,
Stamp, stamp, just like that?

Can you take some great big strides
Just like a giant can?
Or walk along so slowly
Like a poor bent old man?

Anon.

Build a House

Build a house with five bricks,

One, two, three, four, five.

Use your clenched fists for bricks,
putting one on top of the other five times.

Put a roof on top

Raise both your arms above your head
with your fingers touching.

And a chimney, too,

Straighten your arms.

Where the wind blows through . . .

WHOO WHOO!

Blow hard!

Anon.

I'm a Little Teapot

I'm a little teapot, short and stout;
Here's my handle, here's my spout.

*Put one hand on your hip, and hold the other out
like the spout on a teapot.*

When I see the tea-cups, hear me shout,
"Tip me up and pour me out."

*Lean over towards your "spout" arm, as if you're
pouring out tea.*

Anon.

Incey Wincey Spider

Incey Wincey spider
Climbing up the spout;

Use all your fingers to show how the spider climbs up.

Down came the rain
And washed the spider out:

Wriggle your fingers down to show the rain.

Out came the sun
And dried up all the rain;

Sweep your hands up and bring them out and down.

Incey Wincey spider
Climbing up again.

Do the same as for the first line.

Anon.

Flowers Grow Like This

Flowers grow like this,

Cup your hands.

Trees grow like this;

Spread your arms out wide.

I grow
Just like that!

Jump up and stretch.

Anon.

Oliver Twist

Do the actions the rhyme suggests.

Oliver-Oliver-Oliver Twist
Bet you a penny you can't do this:
Number one—touch your tongue.
Number two—touch your shoe.
Number three—touch your knee.
Number four—touch the floor.
Number five—stay alive.
Number six—wiggle your hips.
Number seven—jump to Heaven.
Number eight—bang the gate.
Number nine—walk the line.
Number ten—start again.

Anon.

Quack! Quack! Quack!

Farmyard Poems

If I had a Donkey

If I had a donkey
That wouldn't go
D'you think I'd wallop him?
No! No! No!
I'd put him in a stable
And keep him nice and warm,
The best little donkey
That ever was born.
Gee up, Neddy,
Gee up, Neddy,
The best little donkey
That ever was born.

Anon.

In the Fields

One day I saw a big brown cow
Raise her head and chew,
I said, "Good morning, Mrs Cow,"
But all she said was, "Moo!"

One day I saw a woolly lamb,
I followed it quite far,
I said, "Good morning, little lamb,"
But all it said was, "Baa!"

One day I saw a dappled horse
Cropping in the hay,
I said, "Good morning, Mr Horse,"
But all he said was, "Neigh!"

Anon.

The Prayer of the Little Ducks

Dear God,

give us a flood of water.

Let it rain tomorrow and always.

Give us plenty of little slugs

and other luscious things to eat.

Protect all folk who quack

and everyone who knows how to swim.

Amen.

Carmen Bernos de Gasztold
translated by Rumer Godden

Cow Chat

Mama Moo
Papa Moo
Baby Moo
lying in the grass

Said Mama Moo
to Papa Moo
"When the grass is new
I love to chew"

"And I do too"
said Baby Moo

John Agard

Cock a Doodle Doo!

Cock a doodle doo!
My dame has lost her shoe;
My master's lost his fiddling stick,
And knows not what to do.

Cock a doodle doo!
What is my dame to do?
Till master finds his fiddling stick,
She'll dance without her shoe.

Cock a doodle doo!
My dame has found her shoe,
And master's found his fiddling stick,
Sing doodle doodle doo!

Cock a doodle doo!
My dame will dance with you,
While master fiddles his fiddling stick,
For dame and doodle doo.

Anon.

White Sheep

White sheep, white sheep
On a blue hill,
When the wind stops
You all stand still.
You all run away
When the winds blow;
White sheep, white sheep,
Where do you go?

W. H. Davies

Baa, Baa, Black Sheep

Baa, baa, black sheep,
  Have you any wool?
Yes, sir, yes, sir,
  Three bags full;
One for the master,
  And one for the dame,
And one for the little boy
  Who lives down the lane.

Anon.

Little Boy Blue

Little Boy Blue come blow your horn,

The sheep's in the meadow, the cow's in the corn.

Where is the boy that looks after the sheep?

He's under a haycock fast asleep.

Will you wake him? No, not I!

For if I do, he's sure to cry.

Anon.

Pick, Crow, Pick

Pick, crow, pick, and have no fear,
I sit here and I don't care.
If my master chance to come,
You must fly and I must run.

Anon.

I had a Little Hen

I had a little hen,
The prettiest ever seen,
She washed me the dishes
And kept the house clean.

She went to the mill
To fetch me some flour,
She brought it home
In less than an hour.

She baked me my bread,
She brewed me my ale,
She sat by the fire
And told many a fine tale.

Anon.

A Little Talk

The big brown hen and Mrs Duck
Went walking out together;
They talked about all sorts of things—
The farmyard, and the weather.
But all I heard was: "Cluck! Cluck! Cluck!"
And "Quack! Quack! Quack!" from Mrs Duck.

Anon.

The Pasture

I'm going out to clean the pasture spring;
I'll only stop to rake the leaves away
(And wait to watch the water clear, I may):
I sha'n't be gone long.—You come too.

I'm going out to fetch the little calf
That's standing by the mother. It's so young
It totters when she licks it with her tongue.
I sha'n't be gone long.—You come too.

Robert Frost

Slowly

Slowly the tide creeps up the sand,
Slowly the shadows cross the land.
Slowly the cart-horse pulls his mile,
Slowly the old man mounts the stile.

Slowly the hands move round the clock,
Slowly the dew dries on the dock.
Slow is the snail—but slowest of all
The green moss spreads on the old brick wall.

James Reeves

Six Little Ducks

Six little ducks that I once knew,
Fat ones, skinny ones, they were too;
But the one little duck with
    the feathers on his back,
He ruled the others with his
    "Quack, quack, quack!
    Quack, quack, quack!"
He ruled the others with his
    "Quack, quack, quack!"

Down to the river they would go,
Wibble, wobble, wibble, wobble, to and fro;
But the one little duck with
    the feathers on his back,
He ruled the others with his
    "Quack, quack, quack!
    Quack, quack, quack!"
He ruled the others with his
    "Quack, quack, quack!"

Home from the river they would come,
Wibble, wobble, wibble, wobble, ho-hum-hum;
But the one little duck with
    the feathers on his back,
He ruled the others with his
    "Quack, quack, quack!
    Quack, quack, quack!"
He ruled the others with his
    "Quack, quack, quack!"

Anon.

Lamplighter Barn

I can play
in the prickly hay
and I can find
where the chickens lay
and take off my shoes
and stay
and stay
in the tickly hay
on a rainy day.

Myra Cohn Livingston

Jack and Jill

Jack and Jill went up the hill,
    To fetch a pail of water;
Jack fell down, and broke his crown,
    And Jill came tumbling after.

Anon.

Quack, Quack!

We have two ducks. One blue. One black.
And when our blue duck goes "Quack-quack"
our black duck quickly quack-quacks back.
The quacks Blue quacks make her quite a quacker
but Black is a quicker quacker-backer.

Dr Seuss

Hickety, Pickety, my Black Hen

Hickety, pickety, my black hen,
She lays eggs for gentlemen;
Gentlemen come every day,
To see what my black hen doth lay.
Some days five and some days ten,
She lays eggs for gentlemen.

Anon.

Bow-Wow, Says the Dog

Bow-wow, says the dog,
Mew, mew, says the cat,
Grunt, grunt, goes the hog,
And squeak goes the rat.
Tu-whu, says the owl,
Caw, caw, says the crow,
Quack, quack, says the duck,
And what cuckoos say you know.

Anon.

Do Your Ears Hang Low?

Nonsense Poems and
Tongue-Twisters

What's in There?

What's in there?
   Gold and money.
Where's my share of it?
   The mouse ran away with it.
Where's the mouse?
   In her house.

Where's her house?
   In the wood.
Where's the wood?
   The fire burnt it.
Where's the fire?
   The water quenched it.

Where's the water?
  The brown bull drank it.
Where's the brown bull?
  At the back of Birnie's Hill.
Where's Birnie's Hill?
  All clad with snow.
Where's the snow?
  The sun melted it.
Where's the sun?
  High, high up in the air.

Anon.

Peter Piper

Peter Piper picked a peck of pickled pepper;
Did Peter Piper pick a peck of pickled pepper?
If Peter Piper picked a peck of pickled pepper,
Where's the peck of pickled pepper
Peter Piper picked?

Anon.

Down the Slippery Slide

Down the slippery slide they slid
Sitting slightly sideways;
Slipping swiftly see them skid
On holidays and Fridays.

Anon.

Betty Botter

Betty Botter bought some butter,
But, she said, this butter's bitter;
If I put it in my batter,
It will make my batter bitter,
But a bit of better butter
Will make my batter better.
So she bought a bit of butter
Better than her bitter butter,
And she put it in her batter,
And it made her batter better,
So 'twas better Betty Botter
Bought a bit of better butter.

Anon.

Kittens with Mittens

Where are you going,
My little kittens?

We are going to town
To get us some mittens.

What! mittens for kittens!
Do kittens wear mittens?
Who ever saw little kittens with mittens?

Anon.

A Hat for a Cat

Where are you going,
My little cat?

I am going to town,
To get me a hat.

What! a hat for a cat!
A cat get a hat!
Who ever saw a cat with a hat?

Anon.

Nobody Loves Me

Nobody loves me,
Everybody hates me,
I think I'll go and eat worms.

Big fat squishy ones,
Little thin skinny ones,
See how they wriggle and squirm.

Bite their heads off.
"Schlurp!" they're lovely,
Throw their tails away.

Nobody knows
How big I grows
on worms three times a day.

Anon.

Wish I was a Little Grub

Wish I was a little grub
with whiskers round my tummy.
I'd climb into a honey-pot
and make my tummy gummy.

Anon.

Anna Maria

Anna Maria she sat on the fire;
The fire was too hot, she sat on the pot;
The pot was too round, she sat on the ground;
The ground was too flat, she sat on the cat;
The cat ran away with Maria on her back.

Anon.

Tickly, Tickly

Tickly, tickly, on your knee,
If you laugh you don't love me.

Anon.

Doctor Stickles

Dr Stickles tickled me
And I began to giggle.
Dr Stickles tickled harder
Then I began to wiggle.
When Dr Stickles tickled my toes
I laughed and so would you.
Then I tickled Dr Stickles
Because he was ticklish, too!

Sheree Fitch

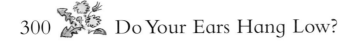

Do Your Ears Hang Low?

Do your ears hang low?

Do they wobble to and fro?

Can you tie them in a knot?

Can you tie them in a bow?

Can you throw them over your shoulder

Like a regimental soldier?

Do your ears hang low?

Anon.

Bananas

Bananas,

In pyjamas,

Are coming down the stairs;

Bananas,

In pyjamas,

Are coming down in pairs;

Bananas,

In pyjamas,

Are chasing teddy bears—

'Cos on Tuesdays

They all try to

CATCH THEM UNAWARES

Carey Blyton

There was a Crooked Man

There was a crooked man,
    And he walked a crooked mile,
He found a crooked sixpence
    Against a crooked stile;
He bought a crooked cat,
    Which caught a crooked mouse,
And they all lived together
    In a little crooked house.

Anon.

Rub-a-Dub-Dub

Rub-a-dub-dub,
Three men in a tub,
And who do you think they be?
The butcher, the baker,
The candlestick-maker,
Turn 'em out, knaves all three.

Anon.

Hey Diddle Diddle

Hey diddle diddle,

The cat and the fiddle,

The cow jumped over the moon;

The little dog laughed

To see such sport,

And the dish ran away

With the spoon.

Anon.

Pop Goes the Weasel!

Up and down the City Road,
    In and out the Eagle,
That's the way the money goes,
    Pop goes the weasel!

A ha'penny for a cotton ball,
    A farthing for a needle,
That's the way the money goes,
    Pop goes the weasel!

Half a pound of tuppeny rice,
    Half a pound of treacle,
Mix it up and make it nice,
    Pop goes the weasel!

Anon.

Tweedledum and Tweedledee

Tweedledum and Tweedledee
    Agreed to have a battle,
For Tweedledum said Tweedledee
    Had spoiled his nice new rattle.
Just then flew by a monstrous crow,
    As big as a tar-barrel,
Which frightened both the heroes so,
    They quite forgot their quarrel.

Anon.

The North Wind Doth Blow

Poems about the Weather

On Mayday

On Mayday we dance,
On Mayday we sing,
For this is the day
We welcome the Spring.

Anon.

Nicely, Nicely

Nicely, nicely, nicely, away in the east,
the rain clouds care for the little corn plants
as a mother cares for her baby.

Zuni Corn Ceremony

Spring

Sound the flute!
Now 'tis mute;
Birds delight
Day and night
Nightingale
In the dale;
Lark in the sky
Merrily,
Merrily, merrily to welcome in the year.

Little boy,
Full of joy;
Little girl,
Sweet and small;
Cock does crow,
So do you;
Merry voice
Infant noise;
Merrily, merrily to welcome in the year.

Little lamb,
Here I am;
Come and lick
My white neck;
Let me pull
Your soft wool;
Let me kiss
Your soft face;
Merrily, merrily we welcome in the year.

William Blake

August Heat

In August, when the days are hot,
I like to find a shady spot,
And hardly move a single bit—
And sit—

    And sit—

        And sit—

            And sit!

Anon.

sun

The sun
Is a leaping fire
Too hot
To go near,

But it will still
Lie down
In warm yellow squares
On the floor

Like a flat
Quilt, where
The cat can curl
And purr.

Valerie Worth

My New Umbrella

I have a new umbrella,
A bright red new umbrella,
A new red silk umbrella,
I wish that it would rain,

And then I could go walking,
Just like a lady walking,
A grown-up lady walking
Away 'way down the lane.

I could not step in puddles,
The shiny tempting puddles,
No lady walks in puddles,
Then turn, and home again.

M. M. Hutchinson

The Rain

Rain on the green grass,
   And rain on the tree,
And rain on the house-top.
   But not upon me!

Anon.

Haiku: winter downpour.

Winter downpour—
even the monkey
needs a raincoat.

Basho
(translated by Lucien Stryk)

The Leaves are Green

The leaves are green
The nuts are brown,
They hang so high
They will not come down.

Leave them alone
Till frosty weather,
Then they will all
Come down together.

Anon.

Autumn

Yellow the bracken,
　　Golden the sheaves,
Rosy the apples,
　　Crimson the leaves;
Mist on the hillside,
　　Clouds grey and white.
Autumn, good morning!
　　Summer, good night!

Florence Hoatson

The Garden Year

January brings the snow,
Makes our feet and fingers glow.

February brings the rain,
Thaws the frozen lake again.

March brings breezes loud and shrill,
Stirs the dancing daffodil.

April brings the primrose sweet,
Scatters daisies at our feet.

May brings flocks of pretty lambs,
Skipping by their fleecy dams.

June brings tulips, lilies, roses,
Fills the children's hands with posies.

Hot July brings cooling showers,
Apricots and gillyflowers.

August brings the sheaves of corn,
Then the harvest home is borne.

Warm September brings the fruit,
Sportsmen then begin to shoot.

Fresh October brings the pheasant,
Then to gather nuts is pleasant.

Dull November brings the blast,
Then the leaves are whirling fast.

Chill December brings the sleet,
Blazing fire, and Christmas treat.

Sara Coleridge

Happiness

John had
Great Big
Waterproof
Boots on;
John had a
Great Big
Waterproof
Hat;
John had a
Great Big
Waterproof
Mackintosh—
And that
(Said John)
Is
That.

A.A. Milne

All Day Saturday

Let it sleet on Sunday,
Monday let it snow,
Let the mist on Tuesday
From the salt-sea flow.
Let it hail on Wednesday,
Thursday let it rain,
Let the wind on Friday
Blow a hurricane,
But Saturday, Saturday
Break fair and fine
And all day Saturday
Let the sun shine.

Charles Causley

The North Wind Doth Blow

The north wind doth blow,
And we shall have snow,
And what will poor robin do then,
Poor thing?
He'll sit in a barn,
And keep himself warm,
And hide his head under his wing,
Poor thing!

Anon.

Brooms

On stormy days
When the wind is high,
Tall trees are brooms
Sweeping the sky.

They swish their branches
In buckets of rain
And swash and sweep it
Blue again.

Dorothy Aldis

Thoughts for a Cold Day

A little bit of blowing,
   A little bit of snow,
A little bit of growing,
   And crocuses will show;
On every twig that's lonely
   A new green leaf will spring;
On every patient tree-top
   A thrush will stop and sing.

Anon.

Snow

Feathery soft and quiet the snow;
It covers the road
    and the walk
    and the rooftops
    and whispers to the world:
                  Shhh!

Margaret R. Moore

Dragon Smoke

Breathe and blow
white clouds
   with every puff.
It's cold today,
   cold enough
to see your breath.
Huff!
   Breathe dragon smoke
    today!

Lilian Moore

Don't go Looking for Fairies

*Magical
and Spooky Poems*

Countdown

There are ten ghosts in the pantry,
There are nine upon the stairs,
There are eight ghosts in the attic,
There are seven on the chairs,
There are six within the kitchen,
There are five along the hall,
There are four upon the ceiling,
There are three upon the wall,
There are two ghosts on the carpet,
Doing things that ghosts will do,
There is one ghost right behind me
Who is oh so quiet . . . BOO!

Jack Prelutsky

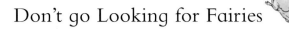

Three Little Ghostesses

Three little ghostesses,
Sitting on postesses,
Eating buttered toastesses,
Greasing their fistesses,
Up to the wristesses,
Oh, what beastesses
To make such feastesses!

Anon.

A Fairy Went A-Marketing

A fairy went a-marketing—
　　She bought a little fish;
She put it in a crystal bowl
　　Upon a golden dish.
An hour she sat in wonderment
　　And watched its silver gleam,
And then she gently took it up
　　And slipped it in a stream.

A fairy went a-marketing—
　　She bought a coloured bird;
It sang the sweetest, shrillest song
　　That ever she had heard.
She sat beside its painted cage
　　And listened half the day,
And then she opened wide the door
　　And let it fly away.

A **fairy** went a-marketing—
    She bought a winter gown
All stitched about with gossamer
    And lined with thistledown.
She wore it all the afternoon
    With prancing and delight,
Then gave it to a little frog
    To keep him warm at night.

A fairy went a-marketing—
    She bought a gentle mouse
To take her tiny messages,
    To keep her tiny house.
All day she kept its busy feet
    Pit-patting to and fro,
And then she kissed its silken ears,
    Thanked it, and let it go.

Rose Fyleman

The Man in the Moon

The man in the moon
Came down too soon,
And asked his way to Norwich;
He went by the south,
And burnt his mouth
With supping cold plum porridge.

Anon.

There was an Old Woman Tossed Up in a Basket

There was an old woman tossed up in a basket,
    Seventeen times as high as the moon;
And where she was going, I couldn't but ask it,
    For in her hand she carried a broom.
Old woman, old woman, old woman, quoth I,
    O whither, O whither, O whither so high?
To sweep the cobwebs off the sky!
    Shall I go with you? Aye, by-and-by.

Anon.

The Little Elf-Man

I met a little elf-man once
Down where the lilies blow.
I asked him why he was so small,
And why he didn't grow.

He slightly frowned, and with his eye
He looked me through and through—
"I'm just as big for me," said he,
"As you are big for you!"

J. K. Bangs

Fairies

Don't go looking for fairies,
  They'll fly away if you do.
You never can see the fairies
  Till they come looking for you.

Eleanor Farjeon

Danger

Large red dragons
Are dangerous.
But small, pretty
Pink ones are usually
Only
Pretending.

Irene Yates

The Lonely Dragon

A dragon is sad

Because everyone thinks

A dragon is fierce and brave,

And roars out flames,

And eats everybody,

Whoever comes near his cave.

But a dragon likes people,

A dragon needs friends,

A dragon is lonely and sad,

If anyone knows

Of a friend for a dragon,

A dragon would be very glad.

Theresa Heine

The Fairy Sleep and Little Bo-Peep

Little Bo-Peep,

Had lost her sheep,

And didn't know where to find them,

All tired she sank

On a grassy bank,

And left the birds to mind them.

Then the fairy, Sleep,

Took little Bo-Peep,

In a spell of dreams he bound her,

And silently brought

The flock she sought,

Like summer clouds around her.

When little Bo-Peep—
In her slumber deep—
Saw lambs and sheep together,
All fleecy and white,
And soft and light,
As clouds in July weather;

Then little Bo-Peep
Awoke from her sleep,
And laughed with glee to find them
Coming home once more,
The old sheep before,
And the little lambs behind them.

Anon.

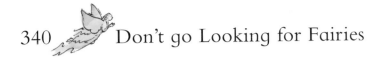

The Dark Wood

In the dark, dark wood,
    there was a dark, dark house,
And in that dark, dark house,
    there was a dark, dark room,
And in that dark, dark room,
    there was a dark, dark cupboard,
And in that dark, dark cupboard,
    there was a dark, dark shelf,
And on that dark, dark shelf,
    there was a dark, dark box,
And in that dark, dark box there was a
GHOST!

Anon.

Bedtime Stories

"Tell me a story,"
Says Witch's Child.
"About the Beast
So fierce and wild.
About a Ghost
That shrieks and groans.
A Skeleton
That rattles bones.
About a Monster
Crawly-creepy.
Something nice
To make me sleepy."

Lilian Moore

Some One

Some one came knocking
  At my wee, small door;
Some one came knocking,
  I'm sure—sure—sure;
I listened, I opened,
  I looked to left and right,
But nought there was a-stirring
  In the still dark night;
Only the busy beetle
  Tap-tapping in the wall,
Only from the forest
  The screech-owl's call,
Only the cricket whistling
  While the dewdrops fall,
So I know not who came knocking,
  At all, at all, at all.

Walter de la Mare

Star Light,
Star Bright

Poems for Bedtime

Go to Bed, Tom

Go to bed, Tom,
Go to bed, Tom,
Tired or not, Tom,
Go to bed, Tom.

Anon.

Go to Bed Late

Go to bed late,
Stay very small;
Go to bed early,
Grow very tall.

Anon.

Bed-time

The evening is coming,
The sun sinks to rest;
The rooks are all flying
Straight home to the nest.
"Caw!" says the rook, as he flies overhead;
"It's time little people were going to bed!"

The flowers are closing;
The daisy's asleep;
The primrose is buried
In slumber so deep.
Shut up for the night is the pimpernel red;
It's time little people were going to bed!

The butterfly, drowsy,
Has folded its wing;
The bees are returning,
No more the birds sing.
Their labour is over, their nestlings are fed;
It's time little people were going to bed!

Anon.

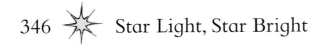

The Mouse's Lullaby

Oh, rock-a-by, baby mouse, rock-a-by, so!
When baby's asleep to the baker's I'll go,
And while he's not looking I'll pop from a hole,
And bring to my baby a fresh penny roll.

Palmer Cox

Star Wish

Star light, star bright,
First star I see tonight,
I wish I may, I wish I might,
Have the wish I wish tonight.

Anon.

The Star
(extract)

Twinkle, twinkle, little star,
How I wonder what you are!
Up above the world so high,
Like a diamond in the sky.

Jane Taylor

Dormouse

"Now Winter is coming,"
The dormouse said,
"I must be thinking
Of going to bed."
So he curled himself up
As small as he could,
And went fast asleep
As a dormouse should.

Lilian McCrea

Flowers at Night

Some flowers close their petals,
blue and red and bright,
and go to sleep all tucked away
inside themselves at night.

Some flowers leave their petals
like windows open wide
so they can watch the goings-on
of stars and things outside.

Aileen Fisher

Wee Willie Winkie

Wee Willie Winkie
Runs through the town,
Upstairs and downstairs
In his night-gown,
Rapping at the window,
Crying through the lock,
Are the children all in bed,
For now it's eight o'clock?

Anon.

Goosey, Goosey Gander

Goosey, goosey gander,
  Whither shall I wander?
Upstairs and downstairs
  And in my lady's chamber.
There I met an old man
  Who would not say his prayers,
I took him by the left leg
  And threw him down the stairs.

Anon.

Rub a Dub Dub

Rub a dub dub,

Three babes in a tub

And who do you think got wet?

The daddy, the mummy,

The teddy bear's tummy,

So

    Hoppity

        Out

           You

             GET!

Lucy Coats

After a Bath

After my bath
I try, try, try
to wipe myself
till I'm dry, dry, dry.

Hands to wipe
and fingers and toes
and two wet legs
and a shiny nose.

Just think how much
less time I'd take
if I were a dog
and could shake, shake, shake.

Aileen Fisher

Littlemouse

Light of day going,
Harvest moon glowing,
People beginning to snore,
Tawny owl calling,
Dead of night falling,
Littlemouse opening her door.

Scrabbling and tripping,
Sliding and slipping,
Over the ruts of the plough,

Under the field gate,
Mustn't arrive late,
Littlemouse hurrying now.

Into a clearing,
All the birds cheering,
Woodpecker blowing a horn,
Nightingale fluting,
Blackbird toot-tooting,
Littlemouse dancing till dawn.

Soon comes the morning,
No time for yawning,
Home again Littlemouse creeps,
Over the furrow,
Back to her burrow,
Into bed. Littlemouse sleeps.

Richard Edwards

Silverly

Silverly,
 Silverly,
Over the
 Trees
The moon drifts
 By on a
Runaway
 Breeze.

Dozily,
 Dozily,
Deep in her
 Bed,
A little girl
 Dreams with the
Moon in her
 Head.

Dennis Lee

Charity Chadder

Charity Chadder
Borrowed a ladder,
Leaned it against the moon,
Climbed to the top
Without a stop
On the 31st of June,
Brought down every single star,
Kept them all in a pickle jar.

Charles Causley

Covers

Glass covers windows
    to keep the cold away
Clouds cover the sky
    to make a rainy day

Nighttime covers
    all the things that creep
Blankets cover me
    when I'm asleep

Nikki Giovanni

Hush-a-Bye, Baby

Hush-a-bye, baby,
On the tree top,
When the wind blows
The cradle will rock;
When the bough breaks
The cradle will fall,
Down will come baby,
Cradle, and all.

Anon.

Flying

I saw the moon,
One windy night,
Flying so fast—
All silvery white—
Over the sky
Like a toy balloon
Loose from its string—
A runaway moon.
The frosty stars
Went racing past,
Chasing her on
Ever so fast.
Then everyone said,
"It's the clouds that fly,
And the stars and moon
Stand still in the sky."

But I don't mind—
I saw the moon
Sailing away
Like a toy
Balloon.

J. M. Westrup

I See the Moon

I see the moon,
    And the moon sees me;
God bless the moon,
    And God bless me.

Anon.

That's What We'd Do

If you were an owl,
And I were an owl,
And this were a tree,
   And the moon came out,
I know what we'd do.
We would stand, we two,
On a bough of the tree;
You'd wink at me,
And I'd wink at you;
That's what we'd do,
   Beyond a doubt.

I'd give you a rose
For your lovely nose,
And you'd look at me
    Without turning about.
I know what we'd do
(That is, I and you);
Why, you'd sing to me,
And I'd sing to you;
That's what we'd do,
    When the moon came out.

Mary Mapes Dodge

And That's All

A happy day
Is precious to keep
So take it to bed
And wrap it in sleep.

Max Fatchen

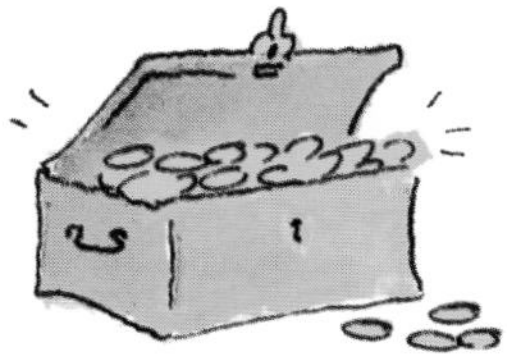

Index of Poems

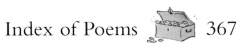

Index of First Lines

Index of Poets

Acknowledgements

The publishers wish to thank the following for permission to use copyright material:

John Agard, 'Cow Chat' and 'Pumpkin Pumpkin' from *No Hickory, No Dickory, No Dock*, Penguin Books, by permission of Caroline Sheldon Literary Agency on behalf of the author, and 'Ask Mummy Ask Daddy' from *I Din Do Nuttin*, Bodley Head, by permission of Random House UK; **Dorothy Aldis**, 'Brooms', 'Everybody Says' and 'Little' from *Everything and Anything*, Copyright © 1925-1927, 1953-1955 by Dorothy Aldis, by permission of G P Putnam's Sons, a division of Penguin Putnam Inc; **Barbara Baker**, 'Spike of Green', by permission of B. Custance Baker; **Basho**, 'Haiku: winter downpour' from *On Love and Barley: Haiku of Basho*, trans. Lucien Stryk, Penguin Classics, 1985. Copyright © Lucien Stryk 1985, by permission of Penguin UK; **Hilaire Belloc**, 'The Elephant' from *Cautionary Verses*, Random House UK, by permission of The Peters Fraser and Dunlop Group Ltd on behalf of the Estate of the author; **Leila Berg**, 'A Garden' from *Time for One More*, Methuen Children's Books, by permission of Reed Consumer Books Ltd; **Valerie Bloom**, 'Water Everywhere', by permission of the author; **Carey Blyton**, 'Bananas' from *Bananas in Pyjamas*, ABC Books, 1994, by permission of the Australian Broadcasting Corporation; **N. M. Bodecker**, 'Hippopotamus' from *Snowman Sniffles*. Copyright © 1983 N. M. Bodecker, by permission of Faber and Faber Ltd and Margaret K. McElderry Books, an imprint of Simon & Schuster Children's Publishing Division; **Ann Bonner**, 'Mud', included in *Twinkle, Twinkle, Chocolate Bar*, John Foster, ed., Oxford University Press, 1991, by permission of the author; **Tony Bradman**, 'I Can Put My Socks On' from *A Kiss on the Nose*, William Heinemann, 1984, by permission of Reed Consumer Books Ltd; **Charles Causley**, 'All Day Saturday', 'Charity Chadder' and 'Spin Me a Web, Spider' from *Collected Poems for Children*, Macmillan Children's Books, by permission of David Higham Associates on behalf of the author; **John Ciardi**, 'What Someone Said When He Was Spanked On the Day Before His Birthday' from *You Know Who*, 1964, by permission of the Ciardi family; **Rebecca Clark**, 'Penguin' from *Cadbury's Ninth Book of Children's Poetry*, 1991, by permission of Cadbury Ltd; **Lucy Coats**, 'Rub a Dub Dub' and 'Waking Up' from *First Rhymes*, Orchard Books, by permission of the Watts Publishing Group; **Myra Cohn Livingston**, 'Lamplighter Barn' from *Wide Awake and Other Poems*. Copyright © 1959, 1987 Myra Cohn Livingston, by permission of Marian Reiner on behalf of the Estate of the author; **Pie Corbett**, 'Ice Lolly', included in *Another Very First Poetry Book*, Oxford University Press, by permission of the author; **W. H. Davies**, 'White Sheep' from *Collected Poems*, Jonathan Cape, by permission of Random House UK on behalf of the Executors of the Estate of the author; **Carmen Bernos de Gasztold**, 'The Prayer of the Little Ducks' from *Prayers from the Ark*, trans. Rumer Godden, 1963, by permission of Macmillan Children's Books; **Walter de la Mare**, 'Some One' from *The Complete Poems of Walter de la Mare*, 1969, by permission of the Literary Trustees of the author and The Society of Authors as their representative; **John Drinkwater**, 'The Snail', by permission of Samuel French Ltd on behalf of the Estate of the author; **Richard Edwards**, 'Littlemouse' from *The Word Party*, 1986, by permission of the author; **Eleanor Farjeon**, 'Fairies' and 'Mrs Peck-Pigeon' from *Silver Sand and Snow*, Michael Joseph, by permission of David Higham Associates Ltd on behalf of the Estate of the author; **Max Fatchen**, 'And That's All' from *Peculiar Rhymes and Lunatic Lines*, Orchard Books, by permission of the Watts Publishing Group; **Rachel Field**, 'Skyscrapers' from *Poems*, Macmillan, NY, 1957. Reprinted with the permission of Simon & Schuster Books for Young Readers, an imprint of Simon & Schuster Children's Publishing Division; **Heidi Fish**, 'My Folks' from *Cadbury's Ninth Book of Children's Poetry*, 1991, by permission of Cadbury Ltd; **Aileen Fisher**, 'After a Bath', 'Upside Down' and 'My Puppy' from *Up the Windy Hill*. Copyright © 1953 Abelard Press, renewed © 1981 by Aileen Fisher, 'The Furry Ones' from *Feathered Ones and Furry*. Copyright © 1971 by Aileen Fisher, and 'Flowers at Night' from *In the Woods, In the Meadow, In the Sky*, Charles Scribners. Copyright © 1965 by Aileen Fisher, by permission of Marian Reiner on behalf of the author; **Sheree Fitch**, 'Doctor Stickles' from *Toes in My Nose*. Copyright © 1987 Sheree Fitch, by permission of Doubleday Canada Ltd; **Robert Frost**, 'The Pasture' from *The Poetry of Robert Frost*, ed. Edward Connery Lathem, Jonathan Cape, by permission of Random House UK; **Rose Fyleman**, 'A Fairy Went A-Marketing' from *Fairies and Chimneys*. Copyright © 1918, 1920 by George H. Doran Company, and 'Singing-Time' and 'Mice' from *Fifty-One New Nursery Rhymes*. Copyright © 1931, 1932 by

Doubleday, a division of Bantam Doubleday Dell Publishing Group, Inc, by permission of The Society of Authors as the Literary Representative of the Estate of the author and Doubleday, a division of Bantam Doubleday Dell Publishing Group, Inc; **Nikki Giovanni**, 'Covers' from *Vacation Time*. Copyright © 1980 by Nikki Giovanni, by permission of William Morrow & Company, Inc; **Kenneth Grahame**, 'Ducks' Ditty' from *The Wind in the Willows*. Copyright © The University Chest, Oxford, by permission of Curtis Brown Ltd on behalf of The University Chest, Oxford; **Nigel Gray**, 'My Cat', by permission of the author; **Theresa Heine**, 'The Lonely Dragon' included in *Twinkle Twinkle, Chocolate Bar*, John Foster, ed., Oxford University Press, 1991, and 'Who Is It?', by permission of the author; **Russell Hoban**, 'Egg Thoughts (soft-boiled)' from *Egg Thoughts and Other Frances Songs*, Faber and Faber, by permission of David Higham Associates on behalf of the author; **Mary Ann Hoberman**, 'Brother' and 'Tiger', copyright © 1959, renewed 1987 by Mary Ann Hoberman, 'Yellow Butter', copyright © 1981 by Mary Ann Hoberman, 'Good Morning When It's Morning', copyright © 1974 by Mary Ann Hoberman, from *The Llama Who Had No Pajama*, by permission of Gina Maccoby Literary Agency on behalf of the author and Harcourt Brace & Company; **Langston Hughes**, 'Hope' from *The Collected Poems of Langston Hughes*. Copyright © 1994 by the Estate of Langston Hughes, by permission of David Higham Associates on behalf of the Estate of the author and Alfred A. Knopf Inc; **Ted Hughes**, 'Cow' from *The Cat and the Cuckoo*, by permission of Faber & Faber Ltd; **Lucia and James L. Hymes Jr.**, 'Oodles of Noodles' from *Oodles of Noodles*. Copyright © 1964 by Lucia and James L. Hymes Jr., by permission of Addison Wesley Longman; **Bobbi Katz**, 'Cat Kisses'. Copyright © 1974, revised 1986 Bobbi Katz, by permission of the author; **W. Kingdon-Ward**, 'Buttons' from *Speech Rhymes*, by permission of A & C Black (Publishers) Ltd; **Karla Kuskin**, 'Giraffes Don't Huff' from *Roar and More*. Copyright © 1956, 1990 by Karla Kuskin, by permission of HarperCollins Publishers, Inc; **D. H. Lawrence**, 'Little Fish' from *The Complete Poems of D. H. Lawrence*, ed. V. de Sola Pinto and F. W. Roberts. Copyright © 1964, 1971 by Angelo Ravagli and C. M. Weekley, Executors of the Estate of Frieda Lawrence Ravagli, by permission of Laurence Pollinger Ltd on behalf of the Estate of Frieda Lawrence Ravagli and Viking Penguin, a division of Penguin Putnam Inc; **Dennis Lee**, 'Skyscraper' from *Alligator Pie*, Macmillan of Canada. Copyright © 1974 Dennis Lee, and 'The Kitty Ran Up the Tree' and 'Silverly' from *Jelly Belly*, Macmillan of Canada. Copyright © 1983 Dennis Lee, by permission of Westwood Creative Artists on behalf of the author; **Vachel Lindsay**, 'The Little Turtle' from *The Collected Poems of Vachel Lindsay*. Copyright © 1925 by Macmillan Publishing Company, renewed 1953 by Elizabeth C. Lindsay. Reprinted with the permission of Simon & Schuster. **Doug MacLeod**, 'A Swamp Romp' from *The Garden of Bad Things*, by permission of Penguin Books Australia Ltd; **Michelle Magorian**, 'Hugs' and 'Babies' from *Orange Paw Marks*, Viking, 1991, pp.18, 55. Copyright © Michelle Magorian, 1991, and 'I Won't' from *Waiting for My Shorts to Dry*, Viking Kestrel, p. 31. Copyright © Michelle Magorian, 1989, by permission of Penguin UK and Rogers, Coleridge and White Ltd on behalf of the author; **David McCord**, 'Bananas and Cream' and an extract from 'Five Chants' from *One at a Time*. Copyright © 1956, 1961 by David McCord, by permission of Little, Brown and Company; **Roger McGough**, 'Ticklish' from *Bad, Bad Cats*, Viking and 'Ever See A Shark' from *The Imaginary Menagerie*, Puffin, by permission of Peters Fraser and Dunlop Group Ltd on behalf of the author; **Colin McNaughton**, 'Potty' from *Who's Been Sleeping in My Porridge*. Copyright © 1990 Colin McNaughton, by permission of Walker Books Ltd; **Eve Merriam**, 'Toaster Time' from *There is no Rhyme for Silver*. Copyright © 1962, 1990 Eve Merriam. Reprinted by permission of Marian Reiner; **Spike Milligan**, 'Today I Saw a Little Worm' and 'Down the Stream the Swans All Glide', by permission of Spike Milligan Productions Ltd; **A. A. Milne**, 'The Three Foxes' and 'Happiness' from *When We Were Very Young*, Methuen Children's Books. Copyright © 1924 by E. P. Dutton, renewed 1952 by A. A. Milne, by permission of Reed Consumer Books Ltd and Dutton Children's Books, a division of Penguin Putnam, Inc; **Lilian Moore**, 'Bedtime Stories' from *See My Lovely Poison Ivy*. Copyright © 1975 by Lilian Moore, and 'Dragon Smoke' from *I Feel the Same Way*. Copyright © 1967, 1995 by Lilian Moore, by permission of Marian Reiner on behalf of the author; **Ogden Nash**, 'The Eel' from *Parents Keep Out*. Copyright © 1936 by Ogden Nash, by permission of Little Brown and Company and Curtis Brown Ltd, New York, on behalf of the Estate of the author; **Judith Nicholls**, 'Blue Wellies, Yellow Wellies' and 'Dinosauristory' from *Popcorn Pie*, Mary Glasgow. Copyright © 1988 by Judith Nicholls, and 'To the Sea!' from *Wish You Were Here?*, Oxford University Press. Copyright © 1992 by Judith Nicholls, by permission of the author; **Grace Nichols**, 'Early Country Village Morning' from *Come On Into My*

Tropical Garden, 'Sugarcake Bubble', 'My Parakeet' and 'Brown-River Brown-River' from *No Hickory, No Dickory, No Dock*. Copyright © Grace Nichols 1988, 1991, by permission of Curtis Brown Ltd on behalf of the author; **Brian Patten**, 'Squeezes' from *Gargling With Jelly*, Penguin Books Ltd. Copyright © Brian Patten 1985, by permission of Rogers, Coleridge and White on behalf of the author; **Jack Prelutsky**, 'Countdown' from *It's Halloween*, William Heinemann, by permission of Reed Consumer Books Ltd; **James Reeves**, 'Slowly' from *The Complete Poems for Children*, Heinemann, by permission of Laura Cecil Literary Agency on behalf of the Estate of the author; **Alastair Reid**, 'Squishy Words (to be said when wet)' from *Ounce Dice Trice*, Abacus, 1991; **John Rice**, 'Dufflecoat', by permission of the author; **Michael Rosen**, 'Busy Day' from *You Tell Me* by Michael Rosen and Roger McGough, 1979, by permission of The Peters Fraser and Dunlop Group Ltd on behalf of the author, and 'Who Likes Cuddles?' from *Don't Put the Mustard in the Custard*, André Deutsch Children's Books. Copyright © Michael Rosen 1985, by permission of Scholastic Ltd; **Vyanne Samuels**, 'Daddy' from *Beams*, Methuen Children's Books, 1990, by permission of Reed Consumer Books Ltd; **Clive Sansom**, 'The Postman', by permission of David Higham on behalf of the author; **Carl Saville**, 'Salty Sea' from *Cadbury's Ninth Book of Children's Poetry*, 1991, by permission of Cadbury Ltd; **Dr Seuss**, extract from 'Quack, Quack' from *Oh Say Can You Say*. Copyright © Dr Seuss Enterprises, L P, 1979, by permission of International Creative Management, Inc on behalf of Dr Seuss Enterprises, L P and Random House, Inc; **Monica Shannon**, 'Only My Opinion' from *Goose Grass Rhymes*. Copyright © 1930 by Doubleday, a division of Bantam Doubleday Dell Publishing Group, Inc, by permission of Doubleday, a division of Bantam Doubleday Dell Publishing Group, Inc; **Arnold L. Shapiro**, 'I Speak, I Say, I Talk' from *Once Upon a Time*, Volume 1 of *Childcraft—The How and Why Library*. Copyright © 1996 World Book, Inc; **Shel Silverstein**, 'Tree House' from *Where the Sidewalk Ends*. Copyright © 1974 by Evil Eye Music, Inc, and 'Needles and Pins' from *Falling Up*. Copyright © 1996 by Shel Silverstein, by permission of Edite Kroll Literary Agency, Inc on behalf of the author and HarperCollins Inc; **Stevie Smith**, 'Nipping Pussy's Feet in Fun' and 'Cat Asks Mouse Out' from *The Collected Poems of Stevie Smith*, Penguin Twentieth Century Classics. Copyright © 1972 by Stevie Smith, by permission of James MacGibbon and New Directions Publishing Corp; **Charles Thomson**, 'Up to the Ceiling' included in *Mr Mop Has a Floppy Top*, Stanford Books, by permission of the author; **Celia Warren**, 'Bears' included in *An Armful of Bears*, Catherine Baker, ed., Methuen Children's Books, by permission of the author; **Clive Webster**, 'Giant' included in *Twinkle Twinkle, Chocolate Bar*, John Foster, ed., Oxford University Press, by permission of the author; **Colin West**, 'Geraldine Giraffe' from *The Best of West*, Hutchinson Children's Books, 1990, by permission of the author; **Valerie Worth**, 'sun' from *Small Poems*. Copyright © 1972 by Valerie Worth, by permission of Farrar, Straus & Giroux, Inc; **Irene Yates**, 'Danger', by permission of Laurence Pollinger Ltd on behalf of the author; **W. B. Yeats**, 'To a Squirrel at Kyle-Na-No' from *The Collected Poems of W. B. Yeats*, by permission of A. P. Watt Ltd on behalf of Michael Yeats.

Every effort has been made to trace the copyright holders but if any have been inadvertently overlooked the publishers will be pleased to make the necessary arrangement at the first opportunity.